MW01290057

Particles In A Stream
D-Day And After

Particles In A Stream
D-Day And After

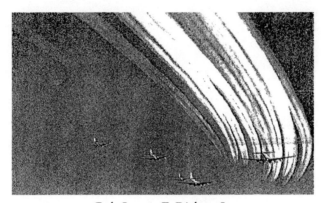

Col. James F. Risher, Jr.
USAF Retired
May 8, 1916-July 22, 1986
Veteran of Eighth USAAF
401st Bomb Group (Heavy)
614th Squadron—"Lucky Devils"

Introduced and Presented by:
James F. Risher III
Joseph K. Risher

James F. Risher Jr.

Copyright © 2012 by James F. Risher Jr.

Library of Congress Control Number:		2011962783
ISBN:	Hardcover	978-1-4691-3785-8
	Softcover	978-1-4691-3784-1
	Ebook	978-1-4653-0616-6

All rights reserved. No part of this book may be reproduced or transmitted in any form or by any means, electronic or mechanical, including photocopying, recording, or by any information storage and retrieval system, without permission in writing from the copyright owner.

This book was printed in the United States of America.

To order additional copies of this book, contact:
Xlibris Corporation
1-888-795-4274
www.Xlibris.com
Orders@Xlibris.com
103433

CONTENTS

Particles in a Stream: D-Day and After
James F. Risher, Jr.
Xlibris, 237 pages, (paperback) $19.99, 9781469137841
(Reviewed: April, 2012)

About halfway through James F. Risher's *Particles in a Stream: D-Day and After*, a present-tense sequence describing a B-17 bombing mission over Germany appears. From waking up at 2:30 in the morning to arriving safely, though flak-punctured, back in England half a day later, the passage can stand with the best writing on aerial combat in World War II.

Immediately after that, reverting to the book's overall past-tense narrative, the story features another excellent section, this one showing readers how officers and airmen spent their down time and dealt with the deaths of friends and the ever-near possibility of their own deaths. Another noteworthy section draws a composite picture of the "average GI pilot" and his attachment to his plane and admiration for its individual "personality."

Most of the story covers the time span between April-August 1944, when Risher was a 27-year-old Army Air Force pilot in the 614th Squadron, 401st Bombardment Group, Eighth Air Force, stationed at Deenthorpe, England. He completed 32 missions and went on to remain in the military for 35 years, dying in 1986. His sons prepared the manuscript for publication.

Risher's account is factual and philosophical at the same time, and not unpleasantly monotonal. The prosaicness of most war remembrances usually dooms them to a limited readership of their authors' families, friends and former comrades. Risher, however, was such a thoughtful, inquisitive person, able to render his observations in lucid writing, that his book can be recommended to anyone wanting a close look at how Americans fought World War II.

Also available in hardcover.

"Interesting descriptions of the author's experience as a B-17 pilot during World War Two. This gripping account of his thirty-two missions from May 1944 through August 1944 offer great insight into the personality of a man for whom commitment to duty was everything. I would highly recommend this book to any history or military buff, or any reader interested in gaining insight into the life of a combat veteran."-Lt. Commander David Pech, U.S. Navy retired aviator.

DEDICATION

➢ To the "Mighty Eighth" Air Force Museum in Savannah, Georgia. For keeping the memory alive.

➢ To Florence "Betty" Risher—a wonderful wife and mother. You could pack up and move an air force family better than anyone.

➢ To Sara Watford, a wonderful sister. Thanks for all the support.

➢ To all who served in the 401st. "The Best Damned Outfit in the USAAF"

➢ To "Skeeter," Lanning, Bill, Gene, and Mary.

FOREWORD

Particles in a Stream is a significant personal account of the United States strategic bombing campaign by the Eighth Army Air Force in the European Theater of World War II. The manuscript was written by Col. James F. Risher, Jr., USAF, retired (born in Smoaks, South Carolina, on May 8, 1916, and died in Atlanta, Georgia, on July 22, 1986). Eleven chapters and the preface were written during his retirement after thirty-five years of military service. Some chapters of the manuscript (chapters 6-11) were found after his death in 1986, which made the whole story complete.

We have included in the last chapter some additional writings in the postwar period during the occupation of Germany. These were found in a file marked "Major J. F. Risher—miscellaneous correspondence and papers." We know these were written between 1948-1950 as he was an air force major at that time, stationed in Germany.

An introduction or foreword was not written by our father. Therefore it is up to the surviving sons to prepare one so the reader will have a historical context of events related to the story.

The time span for most of the story is from April 1944 through August 1944, when the First Lieutenant James F. Risher combat crew flew its thirty-two bombing mission schedule as members of the 401st Bombardment Group based at Deenthorpe, England. The central event during the span of missions was the D-Day invasion by Allied armies—United States, Great Britain, Canada, and others. It is significant that Operation Overlord, the invasion of the Continent of Europe, would not have been possible until the Eighth Air Force was able to gain and maintain air superiority over the German Air Force, along with the Ninth

Tactical Air Force and the Fifteenth Air Force stationed at bases in Italy, and the Royal Air Force, flying nighttime missions to bomb enemy urban areas. The introduction of a long-range fighter airplane that could protect bombers and their defensive formations to and from enemy strategic targets, the North American P-51D Mustang, arrived in large numbers by early 1944. The sleek and serpentine-looking Boeing B-17Gs and the elephantine Consolidated B-24s now had protection throughout their missions, in addition to their own defensive armaments. This was not the case in late 1943, when the Eighth Air Force suffered horrendous losses of bombers and aircrews. Three B-24 Groups of the Eighth were sent to Libya to participate with the Ninth Air Force in the low-level raid on the Ploesti, Romania, oil refineries on August 14, and were badly shot up by enemy antiaircraft weapons and fighter planes. Rebuilding these groups with replacement planes and crews took months. The results of the disastrous Schweinfurt-Regensburg mission in August to destroy enemy ball bearing and aircraft industries, a deadly and unsuccessful raid on Stuttgart on September 6, and a second raid on Schweinfurt in October 1943, were the loss of nearly two hundred bombers destroyed by enemy fighters or radar directed antiaircraft cannons on these three missions alone. Many bombers that returned to bases were too battle damaged to fly again. The British Spitfires, Republic P-47s, and Lockheed P-38s did not have the fuel range to escort the bomber formations on long missions. As a result of these and other devastating setbacks, the Eight Air Force had to stand down from long missions until more bombers, replacement crews, and the long-range fighters arrived by early 1944.

General James H. "Jimmy" Doolittle took command of the Eighth Air Force in January 1944. He changed fighter tactics by allowing them to attack enemy military installations and airfields on the ground, as well as escort the bomber formations. He executed Operation Argument (also known as Big Week) to begin on February 20, 1944, which targeted Germany's key aircraft manufacturing facilities, resulting in greatly reduced enemy fighter strength. The long-range P-51 Mustangs and other allied fighters attacked enemy aircraft that were striking the bomber formations, as well as attacking enemy aircraft on the ground at their bases. The Eighth Air Force also coordinated with the Fifteenth Air Force, Ninth Air Force, and the nighttime-flying Royal Air Force to attack enemy aircraft manufacturing installations. This was a fine example of the Combined Bomber Offensive agreed upon by President Roosevelt and Prime Minister Winston Churchill at the Casablanca conference. Many bombers were lost during Operation Big Week, but enemy aircraft installations were significantly destroyed, and the Germans were not able to replace the many skilled, experienced pilots that were killed. The German Air Force was now hunted in its home. The first steps for the Allied campaign to gain air superiority for the D-Day invasion was complete. The Eighth Air Force would continue to suffer high bomber losses, but it was now prepared to replace crews and aircraft at an overwhelming rate, which the enemy was unable to match by mid-1944. The industrial might of America was winning the deadly war of attrition.

The enemy could not sustain its previous large-scale attacks on the bombers, largely due to its inability to provide seasoned, skilled fighter pilots after Big Week. This operation paved the way for D-Day. The pressure was also on Allied commanders from the Soviet Union, to open the second front on Hitler and the Nazis. This would help the Soviets to crush the German armies in the east (and it also helped the Soviet Communists' hidden agenda of postwar expansion and domination plans).

The airmen of the "Mighty Eighth" paid a high price for their contribution to ending the Second World War. From 1942 to the unconditional surrender of Germany on May 7, 1945, it suffered an estimated 47,000 casualties: 26,000 dead and about 21,000 became POW's or, MIA. The Eighth Air Force had over one-half of all army air force casualties in WWII, and more than any units of the other U.S. fighting forces—army, navy, and marines.

In addition to the long-range high-altitude strategic bombing missions, of which more than one thousand B-17s and B-24s and hundreds of escort fighters were commonly employed by mid-1944, the 401st and other Eighth Air Force groups participated in midlevel attacks on enemy ground forces in support of the D-Day Invasion and the subsequent breakout of Allied ground forces from the Normandy beachheads—Operation Cobra (July 24-26, 1944). For his leadership and aircraft-commander skills during this operation, our father was awarded the Distinguished Flying Cross.

Particles in a Stream is more than a combat diary—it is a narrative of personal impressions and feelings from the prospective of almost two decades after the end of World War II. It concerns how each man on a ten man bomber crew must perform his job and depend on each other and return from a mission alive-and live to fly another day. The story reveals the response of individuals to the growing stress of combat in a high altitude (four to six miles), subzero frigid environment, where men had to perform precise technical skills in confined, unheated spaces, with life maintained by an oxygen tube, while controlling a thirty-ton aircraft packed with explosives in a rigid, precise position within large defensive formations, trailing hundreds of miles over enemy territory, and contend with enemy fighter attacks and radar directed antiaircraft cannon fire (known as flak).

To the men of the Eighth and other air forces, every mission was an invasion of enemy territory. As the J. F. Risher crew slugged though each mission, individuals reacted to combat stress in different ways. The average airman's thoughts about sudden death by midair incineration (or capture by the enemy as a lesser alternative) in the cold, rarified atmosphere tended to transform from initial horror and chilling fear to gradual indifference (acceptance) toward one's own possible destruction.

This gradual change was brought on by repeated experiences of seeing other planes and crews blasted out of the sky, combined with the mounting fatigue, whose weight was added by each successive mission.

Interwoven with the creeping anticipation, dread, and sometimes panic and boredom of high altitude warfare, *Particles in a Stream* still describes many stories of humorous flying events and everyday life on the ground at the bomber bases. Central to the story is the mystery of separate human destinies, intertwined in an enormous vortex of events beyond the ability of any individual control or change by themselves. This theme is apparent in chapter 4 ("D-Day and After"). One aircraft and one ten-man crew was a mere speck among all the soldiers, sailors, airmen, ships, and planes in the enormous conflict in the European Theater—and for that matter, the entire World War.

Particles in a Stream also marvels at the colossal organization of the Eighth Air Force, and for that matter the entire U.S. and Allied military efforts to defeat Germany. The story recognizes the army air force linkage with a huge industrial, military, scientific, and civilian support complex-supplying it through a continuous and unrelenting process of creating aircraft and armaments. The "Mighty Eighth" can be visualized as a giant human cycling and threshing machine, absorbing hundreds of thousands of American citizens from all over the country and sorting, planning, training, indoctrinating, and assigning them as airmen with the knowledge and weapons to conduct an increasingly massive and relentless aerial onslaught, the likes of which we will never see again. From its feeble beginnings in 1942, the Eighth Air Force grew to an organization of about 200,000 airmen and support personnel at its peak—and over three thousand aircraft of all types and forty-two heavy bomber and fighter groups by June 1944. Over 350,000 personnel served in the Mighty Eighth during WW II.

In the first chapter ("Joining"), Lieutenant Risher references the continuous cycle of pilot and crew training so rapidly established by the army air force at the outbreak of WWII—primary, basic, advanced training, and crew training. Many entered pilot training and a large number "washed out" and were assigned other duties. While listening as new arrivals to the 401st Group barracks at Deenthorpe Air Station, combat veterans told him and his newly arrived crew about their mission experiences. He reached a chilling realization: "this was the top, and they (veteran airmen) were still at the top and living the experience. And we did not listen to them with the vibrant expectancy of the newcomer to primary, basic, or advanced training. This was not a matter of live and learn and pass on to the next phase or wash out. This was live, learn, or die."

Particles in a Stream is a strong statement of the interconnection of human destinies within the colossal stage of the Second World War, and the ultimate triumph of good over evil. Since the original manuscript was untitled (identified only as Summer Diary, 1944), we have chosen the title. We have also enhanced our father's basic manuscript with photographs, which help explain and visualize the story. These did not exist in the original manuscript drafts (there was no internet then). As you read the story, we hope the reason for choosing this title will be apparent. We hope you will enjoy *Particles in a Stream*.

James F. Risher III and Joseph K. Risher

PREFACE

The Eighth Air Force, the Strategic Air Force in Europe, fought an isolated aerial warfare. Although the Eighth may not justifiably be called "The Silent Service," in some respects, its operations might be compared to submarine warfare. The similarity is that these two kinds of combat were remote and were removed from any immediate or direct contact with other phases of conflict. Both were inevitably and unmistakably woven into the strategic long-range pattern of the war; neither was directly associated or linked with any other phase by the nature of its activity.

Whereas the Ninth Tactical Air Force—composed of medium bombers, fighter-bombers, and fighters—was created and functioned for close tactical cooperation with the ground forces on the continent, the Eighth Air Force, composed of B-17 and B-24 bombers and fighter aircraft for escort, functioned primarily for the long-range destruction of German targets, in the form of industrial or military installations. Whereas the Ninth in performing its mission leapfrogged from England to France, and then from base to base in France in order to remain close to the scene of action, the Eighth remained fixed at permanent bases in England and continued throughout the war its long-range penetrations. Those occasions when the heavy bombers of the Eighth took part in close support operations were departures from their normal aloof and isolated roles as strategic bombers.

While fighters and fighter-bombers of the Ninth were blowing bridges and destroying trains and transport in the immediate front of the ground forces or destroying airfields and other installations within limited range of the battlefield, the four-engine bombers of the Eighth were flying deep into Germany and striking Munich, Hanover, Peenemunde, Merseburg, Oscherslaben, and Berlin day after day. While the tactical commands, the groups, and the squadrons of the Ninth moved forever forward with the ground forces and lived and fought in the closest proximity to them, the wings and groups of the Eighth remained at their more permanent bases in England and continued the strategic aerial invasions, which had gone on long before D-Day.

The point, of course, is not to claim any particular virtue for this specialized warfare but, rather, to suggest that, by its very nature, it had distinct and singular aspects for the human elements engaged in it—distinct and singular in the sense that most of the extraneous elements contributing to combat fatigue and neurosis were absent.

If medical authorities had decided to establish a laboratory for the study of pure combat stresses upon humans—stresses divorced from the usual contributing factors of continuous fatigue, hunger, exposure, discomforts of weather, and other factors usually associated with ground war—the Eighth Air Force would have been their answer. If they had wanted to study the ultimate effects wrought upon men by repeated intervals of intense weariness and strain, brought about by performance of exacting tasks under conditions of extreme danger and hazard, this was the laboratory. In the Eighth they could, and did, observe men who lived a strange existence divided between security and insecurity; between normal, comfortable living in a friendly land and possible death in a cold, thin atmosphere above an enemy country. A ten hour mission contained all the elements of fatigue and nerve stress that could conceivably be involved in one situation. Yet it was followed by a period of comfortable relaxation on a well-established base in England. In the morning, you were in the midst of battle; in the evening, you were in your own home barracks. The cycle was repeated over and over again until, as medical study and observation had determined, an individual had reached that point where he could no longer function effectively in combat.

This was only one of the many ways of fighting in modern war, and it was an easier way than some. We are not interested here in exaggerating or emphasizing this kind of combat, or in assuming for it any relative importance. It was not all tough, nor all easy, and it depended somewhat upon the individual system as to how well a man stood up under it.

The Eighth Air Force was unique in the history of war. Perhaps never again will such an organization exist. Already, many features of its operations have been outmoded. It may well be that never again will ten men transport explosives through the sub-stratosphere in a bomber, each of them connected to life by the thin line of an oxygen hose. Never again, perhaps, will thousands of young Americans be parceled out in groups of ten to embark upon an interim so foreign to our normal lives—some to die, and some to live and give the experience meaning. Those who survived have been through a great human experience, one not to be had in a normal lifetime.

The planes not expended in this great enterprise are even now being turned to the shapeless metal from which they came, and they will appear again in peaceful forms. The men who flew them and lived have returned to a normal way of life. The experience itself exists only in the minds of those who lived it. We can never feel that it has been put fully into words, but it is right that we should try.

Col. James F. Risher, Jr.
USAF Retired
(b. May 8, 1916-d. July 22, 1986)
401st Bomb Group (Heavy)
614th Squadron—"Lucky Devils"

(written sometime between 1960-1968)

IMAGES

MISSIONS FLOWN (1944)

7 May	Berlin
8 May	Berlin
19 May	Kiel
22 May	Kiel
24 May	Berlin
29 May	Sorau
4 June	Massey, France
6 June	Ver-Sur-Mere, France (Invasion Target, D-Day)
7 June	Falaise, France
10 June	Gael, France
12 June	Vitry—en—Artois
14 June	Le Bourget, Paris
18 June	Hamburg
19 June	Bordeaux
20 June	Hamburg
21 June	Berlin
24 June	Belloy sur Somme, France
25 June	Montbartier, France
4 July	Saumur, France
6 July	Rely, France
7 July	Leipzig
8 July	Mont Louis Femme, France
11 July	Munich
16 July	Munich
18 July	Peenemunde
19 July	Augsburg
24 July	St. Lo, France
25 July	St. Lo, France

4 August	Anklam, Germany
13 August	Elbeuf
16 August	Schkenditz, Germany
24 August	Weimar, Germany

Source: Pilot's Log Book

CHAPTER ONE

JOINING

1-1 Deenthorpe—Boeing B-17G Flying Fortress heavy bombers of the 401st Heavy Bombardment Group at Deenthorpe Air Station, England. B-17 "Duke's Mixture" is in the foreground. The maintenance crew tent is in the foreground to the right.

Picture taken in winter 1945. Courtesy
of 401st Bomb Group Association.

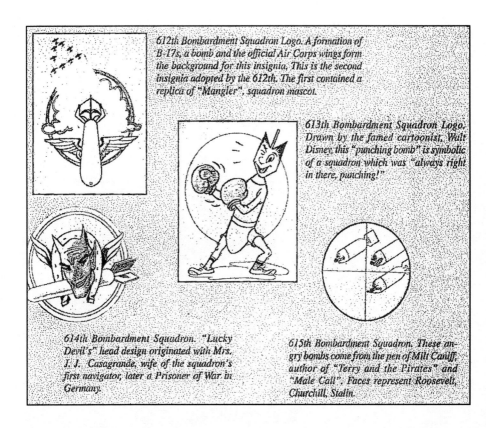

612th Bombardment Squadron Logo. A formation of B-17s, a bomb and the official Air Corps wings form the background for this insignia. This is the second insignia adopted by the 612th. The first contained a replica of "Mangler", squadron mascot.

613th Bombardment Squadron Logo. Drawn by the famed cartoonist, Walt Disney, this "punching bomb" is symbolic of a squadron which was "always right in there, punching!"

614th Bombardment Squadron. "Lucky Devil's" head design originated with Mrs. J. J. Casagrande, wife of the squadron's first navigator, later a Prisoner of War in Germany.

615th Bombardment Squadron. These angry bombs come from the pen of Milt Caniff, author of "Terry and the Pirates" and "Male Call". Faces represent Roosevelt, Churchill, Stalin.

1-2 401st Bomb Group Squadrons. The insignias shown were displayed on bomber crew uniforms proudly. Usually they were patches on uniform shirts and flight jackets.

Source: Courtesy of 401st Bomb Group Association.

1-3 Group Commander—Colonel Harold Bowman was the highly respected 401st Bomb Group (H) Commander in 1944. Col Bowman is shown on the bicycle along side Capt. W.G. McAlexander, an engineering officer

Source: 401st Bomb Group Association

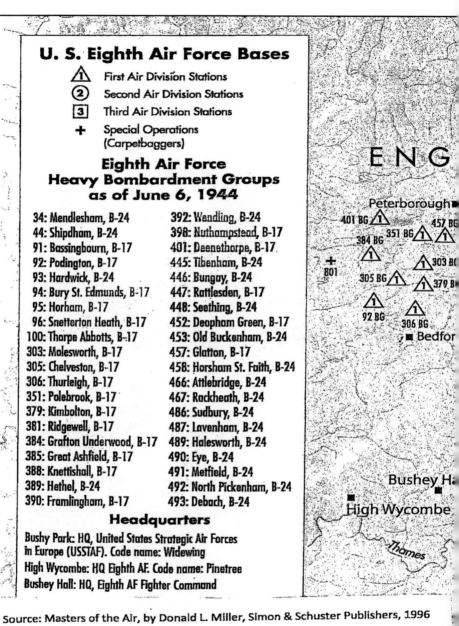

U. S. Eighth Air Force Bases

⚠ First Air Division Stations
② Second Air Division Stations
③ Third Air Division Stations
✛ Special Operations
(Carpetbaggers)

Eighth Air Force
Heavy Bombardment Groups
as of June 6, 1944

34: Mendlesham, B-24	392: Wendling, B-24
44: Shipdham, B-24	398: Nuthampstead, B-17
91: Bassingbourn, B-17	401: Deenethorpe, B-17
92: Podington, B-17	445: Tibenham, B-24
93: Hardwick, B-24	446: Bungay, B-24
94: Bury St. Edmunds, B-17	447: Rattlesden, B-17
95: Horham, B-17	448: Seething, B-24
96: Snetterton Heath, B-17	452: Deopham Green, B-17
100: Thorpe Abbotts, B-17	453: Old Buckenham, B-24
303: Molesworth, B-17	457: Glatton, B-17
305: Chelveston, B-17	458: Horsham St. Faith, B-24
306: Thurleigh, B-17	466: Attlebridge, B-24
351: Polebrook, B-17	467: Rackheath, B-24
379: Kimbolton, B-17	486: Sudbury, B-24
381: Ridgewell, B-17	487: Lavenham, B-24
384: Grafton Underwood, B-17	489: Halesworth, B-24
385: Great Ashfield, B-17	490: Eye, B-24
388: Knettishall, B-17	491: Metfield, B-24
389: Hethel, B-24	492: North Pickenham, B-24
390: Framlingham, B-17	493: Debach, B-24

Headquarters

Bushy Park: HQ, United States Strategic Air Forces
in Europe (USSTAF). Code name: Widewing
High Wycombe: HQ Eighth AF. Code name: Pinetree
Bushey Hall: HQ, Eighth AF Fighter Command

Source: Masters of the Air, by Donald L. Miller, Simon & Schuster Publishers, 1996

1-4 Eighth Air Force Bases—By June 1944, the Eighth U.S. Army Air Force had forty-two groups located throughout England. They were mainly concentrated in the East Anglia area of England.

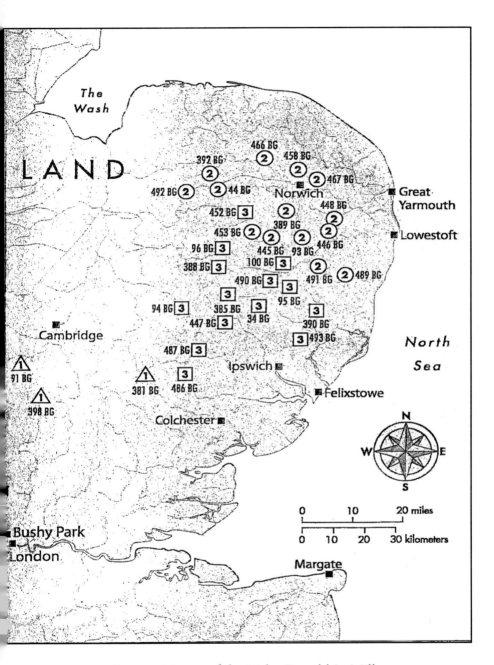

The Wash

LAND

466 BG ②
392 BG ②
458 BG ②
② 467 BG
492 BG ② 44 BG ②
Norwich
448 BG
452 BG 3
②
453 BG ② ②
389 BG ②
② ②
96 BG 3
445 BG 93 BG 446 BG
388 BG 3
100 BG 3
② 489 BG
490 BG 3
3
491 BG ②
3
95 BG
94 BG 3
385 BG 3
3
447 BG 3
34 BG
390 BG
487 BG 3
3 493 BG
Ipswich
North
Sea
△1
91 BG
△1
3
381 BG
486 BG
△1
398 BG
Colchester
Great Yarmouth
Lowestoft
Felixstowe

N
W   E
S

Bushy Park
London

Margate

0   10   20 miles
0   10   20   30 kilometers

Source: *Masters of the Air* by Donald L. Miller,
Simon & Schuster Publishers, 1996.

I. JOINING

A four-hour train trip took us over the last leg of our long journey to combat. We arrived in midafternoon at the ancient town of Kettering. There were five crews on our shipment to the 401st Bomb Group: ourselves and the crews of Lieutenants Opie, Protz, Taylor, and Gillespie. Opie, Protz, Taylor, and I had gone through B-17 transition together at Hendricks Field, Sebring, Florida, and our crews had trained together at Dalhart, Texas. It later developed that three of these new crews were to complete a tour of missions intact. Protz was shot down on the sixth mission, and Gillespie's crew was badly shot up on a later mission—so badly shot up that several members of the crew were grounded for a long time, and the crew did not finish as a unit.

Kettering was a small city with a population of approximately fifteen thousand. Its railroad station was old and dingy as many of ours. There were two ancient hotels, several beautiful old stone churches and several staid parks. In the business district were shops and stores, large and small, neat and dingy. Kettering was to be "our town" by virtue of its location. We went to London, we took the train at Kettering, and we returned to Kettering. And when we left the base between the customary two day passes, it was to go to Kettering for a show.

We piled into the waiting GI trucks and were soon rolling through the outskirts of the town, over a stone bridge, past rows of gray apartment houses and small shops, and out to the rolling countryside. In half an hour, we passed the tiny village of Deenthorpe and found ourselves skirting the edge of the combat base, which was the home of the 401st Bomb Group. We looked out the rear of the trucks at the field and the buildings flashing by.

On certain special occasions in life, very ordinary details stand out with an unusual clarity and significance. There was nothing uncommon about this base—the field itself, the planes scattered around it at their individual dispersal points, or the administrative and barracks buildings clustered in squadron areas. In most respects this field was like the others we had passed through in our movement through England from our initial landing at Nutt's Corner, Ireland, a few weeks ago; and it was not entirely unlike most of the bases on which we had trained back in the States. This was just another airbase; the runways were like all the others we has seen; the control tower, the operations building, the headquarters building, the squadron areas, all these were quite normal in their appearance and arrangement. Yet all these details seemed peculiarly sharp and fresh to me as the truck took us down the highway past the field and in and among the separate areas on our respective squadrons.

Those planes out there on the field were war planes. They had been over enemy territory and dropped bombs, some of them today perhaps. Ground crews worked over them, changing engines, patching fuselages, checking and grooming them. They were fascinating planes at the moment, different from any other we had ever seen. The ambulance and the fire truck sitting by the operations building were something more than customary sights at a flying field. They were there to fill a more frequent need than we had known before. This, by chance, was the one base out of the hundreds on these islands which would be our goal of return from many long missions; this was to be our home while we were engaged in an unusual type of human endeavor, fraught with many dangers, and possible death. It could be that within the next few weeks or months some of us riding on this truck would take to the air from those runways and never touch earth again as living men. It was probable.

We found out that our base was one of the many RAF bases converted for U.S. combat forces. The field itself lay on a level stretch of otherwise rolling countryside. A highway ran just beside it and cultivated fields and farm buildings lay around it on all sides. Group headquarters and administrative buildings were sited nearby, and the four squadron sites lay west of the field in a rough rectangular pattern. They were widely separated. Bicycles and jeeps were the customary ways of getting around. The 614th Squadron, to which we and Taylor's crew were assigned, lay farthest west and was a mile from the field and briefing rooms. Our squadron area merged with a little settlement of stone-and-thatch farmhouses, all very old. There was a little inn nearby with a pub called "The Wheatsheaf."

Jack, Frank, VE, and I were assigned to an officers' barracks across the highway from the main part of the squadron area. It developed that we were sorely needed replacements, for the 614th had lost several crews in the previous week or more.

Our long barracks seemed long indeed. It was occupied only by the four officers of a crew: Connery was the navigator; Fogarty, bombardier; Kelly, copilot; and Wilson, pilot. The men were lonely in their big house and were plainly glad to have company. The inevitable question-and-answer session opened up as we went about the work of moving in. Things, which within three weeks were commonplace to us, were now new and exciting.

As we sat there talking to these men, drinking in their every word, I was impressed more than ever before with the continuous cycle which had been the story of our Air Corps experiences. I remembered only too well that not so many months ago I had sat around a barracks at a primary flying school in Uvalde, Texas, with others of the incoming freshman class and had listened raptly to the words of the seasoned veterans of the class ahead of us. Those veterans had soloed a PT-19 and they were well on their way to basic; they talked about acrobatics, about snap rolls and loops with an easy nonchalance that came only with experiences; and they made us of the new class feel terribly green and inexperienced, which we were. And then, of course, within a matter of a few weeks those of us who had not met hard fate in the "washing machine" (the elimination process) were greeting the newcomers with words of wisdom. We were the veterans and these kids had a lot to learn. We handed down the same old tips which had now passed through several generations of primary students—how to get along with the instructor, how to land the PT in a crosswind, how to outsmart the instructor on simulated forced landings—all these and more we passed along with the proper nonchalance and air of indifference.

And then we went to basic to repeat the cycle, and to advanced, to transition, and finally to operational training—where crews had been banded together and trained. Each time it was a repetition; yet each time it was new. A new plane, new things to learn, stricter requirements, more responsibility; a gradual tightening of the system which surrounded us, so that we were trained and geared psychologically to the job ahead. Each of these two—and three-month periods had been an abbreviated lifetime in itself, a complete experience, a gradual yet rapid development from novice to veteran in a certain type of training. And each period had pointed unerringly to the next. We had been led up a stairway of training, and now we stood on the top of the stairway. The few months ahead would be the inevitable climax. No matter what followed for those who completed a tour, everything else would be lower in the scale.

And though sitting here listening to Wilson and his crew talk as we prodded them was reminiscent of the whole training cycle, there was a subtle but unmistakable difference. These fellows did not talk with the bravado and the practiced nonchalance which had been characteristics of us all in training. They talked in a serious and matter-of-fact way about a serious business. They did not talk with the enthusiasm of men who were finishing with one part of the cycle and hurrying on expectantly to the next and higher part. This was the top and they were still at the top and still living the experience. And we did not listen with the vibrant expectancy of the newcomer to primary or basic or advanced. This was not a matter of live and learn and pass on to the next phase, or wash out; this was live and learn, or die.

Wilson's crew were veterans. They had nineteen missions (with differences of one or two among them), and they had been on some very tough ones. They had been badly shot up twice. Once they had flown back from Oscherslaben on two engines, with most instruments out and no brakes when they landed. Wilson told me that he scarcely remembered what happened for the first few hours after that ordeal; that he was sore and aching for days. On their last mission, a week before, they had come back from Marienburg with a heavily damaged ship and a gravely wounded radio operator. Radio's leg had been amputated. Now the crew had not flown a mission in over a week, and they showed the effects of nervous tension. We missed not the slightest move or gesture of any of them, for to us they were for the present, something in the nature of idols.

On this first afternoon, I asked Fogarty what the normal assignment of a barracks like this was, having noticed that we had more than enough room. His answer was significant.

"It varies," he said simply.

The two crews that had occupied our corner of the long building had been shot down last week. They had, of course, been close friends of these men—close in the ways of barracks friendship at a combat base. They had trained with them and come to England with them. Together they had flown some tough missions and sat out many a dismal winter night of bad weather on the base.

I found several odds and ends of personal equipment as I cleaned out my dresser drawers—stuff of no consequence, which had been left by the adjutant who had gathered the personal effects. But they were reminders of the man, unknown to me, who had slept in my bed and used this dresser only last week, and who was either dead or in a German prison camp. He had lived here full of confidence, believing—as most of us do—that he would live to finish the job and go home. And he had gone a long way. He went down in a spin on his eighth mission. Further reminders were the several neatly stacked boxes in the squadron supply room, labeled MIA. They contained the personal effects of men who had been shot down.

We had made a long journey. Now we had arrived at the time and the place, and these were the visible signs.

The afternoon of arrival, after moving in and becoming acquainted with our barracks mates, I walked over to Fred Taylor's barracks. I found him sitting on a bunk, spellbound. He was listening to the words of one Mike Matritian, another veteran of the 401st and a rather unusual character.

Mike, a first-lieutenant navigator, was a big man. Walsh, his pilot, must have used a lot of elevator trim to keep his nose up with Mike aboard. He was well over six feet and heavy of frame. He had a strong, square, impassive face that made him look older than his twenty-three years. A magnificent handlebar mustache accentuated his settled look. Likewise did the huge pipe with long, curving stem, which he smoked. Between puffs he talked in a low, gentle, confidential tone. He was giving Fred and the other officers of his crew a few highlights of his eighteen missions. Mike was indulging himself in the very natural pastime of impressing the novices with the nature of the game they were about to play with Jerry. And he didn't spare the flak. His words were not lost on Fred and the boys, I could see—or, for that matter, on me.

In these first few days, we learned something of the history of the 401st and absorbed some of its atmosphere. The 401st was one of the younger of the B-17 groups in the Eighth Air Force. It had arrived in England late in November of '43 and had begun operations in December. It had therefore been in action only five months. The group had flown something over fifty missions and had already had replacements. It was just now taking on the aspects of a seasoned combat organization. Very few, if any, of the original crews had yet completed a tour of missions, but some did shortly after we joined. The senior crews were well on their way with from fifteen to twenty missions as the average.

On the walls of the officers' club behind the bar was a neatly printed list of the group missions, showing date and target. Swastikas after the target name showed enemy fighters shot down on the mission. They had been on some rugged ones, particularly in the months of February and March, and there were plenty of swastikas on the wall. The bar itself was carved with many a name and tally of missions. Some of these tally lists were later completed. Some remained unfinished.

Already group legends had arisen, and group traditions. Planes had come back to this base many times damaged beyond belief. This group had its own examples individual courage and unselfishness in the high moments of combat and extreme danger.

We soon heard of the time when one of our ships crashed in the little village of Deenthorpe just after an early morning takeoff; about how fire trucks got over there in nothing flat and saved the village and the crew from being blown out of this world by the load of bombs; how they quickly got all villagers out of bed and out of danger area until the fire was out and the danger past.

We heard of the bombardier, Fogarty by name, who squeezed through the damaged bomb bays of his ship, sans parachute, and went back to give aid to his seriously wounded radio gunner. He stayed back there for four hours with the gunner, whose leg was nearly torn off, while the crippled ship staggered home on two engines. We had not heard this from Fogarty and his crew in that first afternoon's conversation.

Some near tragedies had ended comically. We all know that crew chiefs like to have their crews and planes come home again—but not the way Captain Chapman brought his plane home to its chief. Chapman had led his combat box to Hanover, and his ship was riddled over the target. They fought their way home and somehow managed to get it on the ground. Two engines were out, and they had no brakes. Chapman made a good landing but could not control the ship after she touched down. She careened down the runway. When she finally ground to a stop in the grass, the crew chief's line tent was under the landing gear, and the number four prop hung over his bunk.

There was the time when an enemy FW-190 fighter pilot found himself in an unusual and compromising situation. The group was under heavy fighter attack just after bombing the target. German fighters were coming in from all directions, and fifty calibers were running hot. An FW-190 pilot pulled up from below in attack, miscalculated, and found himself in the middle of the V of the low squadron, practically stalled out. He sat there flying formation with a group of B-17s. He flew there for long moments squarely between the wing ships, the pilot's head swiveling back and forth. The amazed gunners could not fire for fear of blasting their own ships. Should he break away upward and take it from the top turrets, or downward and take it from the ball turrets? It probably didn't make much difference anyway. He ducked, and the ball turrets were waiting. The only question was as to who blasted him out of the sky, and that remained unsettled.

There was the case of Second Lieutenant Kaufman and his bombardier, Second Lieutenant Fitzgerald, flying their ship home on two engines from the target after the other eight members of the crew had bailed out. Kaufman and his crew flew to Emden as element lead of a low squadron on their third mission late in December. The formations encountered intense flak over the target, and Kaufman's ship was knocked out of formation with number three engine dead and number two smoking and losing power. While they fought to bring the ship under control, losing in altitude on their heading for the enemy coast, fire broke out on the wing behind the damaged number two engine. It was time to get out, and Kaufman rang the alarm bell signal to bail out. One by one, and quickly, the crew departed the ship. Kaufman gave the controls to the autopilot, quickly adjusted the elevation control for a gradual descent, and scrambled down into the catwalk for a quick check on all the crew before leaving. He ran head-on into Fitzgerald, who was poised above the nose escape hatch, trying frantically to get his chute adjusted to his harness.

Kaufman groaned and glanced at the wing, expecting it to explode in his face the next instant. Where he expected to see a sheet of flame, there was a thin wisp of smoke. Miraculously, the fire was out. Fitzgerald, still struggling with his chute, looked up desperately and saw what had happened. They looked at each other. Without a word, they scrambled up into the cockpit.

Their troubles were not over. The last hectic ten minutes had left them very uncertain as to their position. They were over a solid overcast and they were flying with half normal power, one engine completely useless and another almost so. They could not sacrifice altitude and go into that overcast until they knew they were over England; yet while they were above it, their whereabouts was an uncertainty. The navigator's map gave them the heading for home and, fortunately, Kaufman had carefully noted the wind direction and velocity at briefing. They established a course and nursed their crippled plane along, constantly adjusting power settings, squeezing all available power from the ailing number two engine. Fitzgerald measured distance on the map with the width of his thumb. The channel was twenty miles wide at a point; he measured it and laid off the distance from Emden to home with his thumb as the instrument. They made a calculation based on wind direction and velocity, time over target, and distance as measured by thumb. An hour and a half later, they ducked into and through the overcast and found themselves over land that looked like England. Soon a British fighter came up and tolled them in for a landing on a training base.

They failed in all attempts to contact the home base to advise of their whereabouts, and it was several days before they were able to put in an appearance at Deenthorpe. The surprise was mutual. Kaufman and Fitzgerald found all their personal effects in the squadron supply room, neatly boxed and labeled for shipment home.

*   *   *

We went to school again for one week. You never get completely away from that. We heard again many of the things we had heard before, but we got a few new things too. It was a break for new crews to attend this group school. Aside from the information imparted, it gave crews time to get their feet planted in the new organization. At the end of the first week, we knew practically everyone we would be associated with during our stay. We knew Major "Pop" Frye—the genial, popular, and hardworking group S2 (Intelligence Officer). We knew Colonel Bowman, group commander; Colonel Brooks, executive officer; Colonel Seawell, air executive officer; and other officers of the groups staff. And we knew Colonel Hinkle, squadron commander of the 614th Squadron; Major Garland, operations officer; and others with whom we would work closely in the months ahead.

The sergeants moved into the squadrons all the way. Harry Baker had established himself in the cleaning and pressing business three days after arrival. He had a homemade ironing board and all necessary accessories. He operated our cleaning service from then on and specialized in quick press jobs—subject, of course, to exigencies of the service (in this case, the regularity of our combat missions).

New crews flew practice missions during this school period. Members were checked in their various capacities. Perhaps there was a special emphasis on checking the new pilots on their formation flying. We also had a couple of "dry runs" on getting between inexperience and jitters, and we had a rough time getting ready for the first few missions. The hour and a half allowed between briefing and takeoff was more than enough for experienced crews. Most of them had their ships ready in half the time and spent the rest of it piddling or, more likely, dozing. But new gunners worked practically the whole time and were often jamming in the last parts as the pilot started engines. Therefore, under the supervision of a veteran crew, the gunners went through the routine of cleaning and installing their guns, checking turrets and connections, and feeding ammunition into place for firing. Our gunners were good, and they checked out very well. However, they found that the job of readying the ship for a combat mission was a little more work than they had thought. And on the first few missions, with knots in their stomachs, they were to find it harder still.

Finally came the morning when we flew as "spare, spare." We carried out no bombs, and we did not attend briefing. We simply got up and ate breakfast with the combat crews, installed guns and ammunition for practice, took off behind the mission, and followed the formation to the English coast. The five new crews were on this flight. So far as combat flying was concerned, this was the first short staggering flight after a considerable amount of hopping about from limb to limb around the nest. When we landed, we knew we had the last "dry run." Tomorrow we would be booted out for good. The next flight would be a mission.

Three days later, Fred Taylor and his crew landed—or rather, fell—on an emergency strip in South England after fighting their way back on the deck from their second trip to Berlin with one engine out, a second giving half power, one man wounded, and the ship full of holes. They were definitely out of the nest. They had been transformed from novices to veterans in two easy lessons.

CHAPTER TWO

THE FIRST FIVE

2-1 Flying Fortress—The G model of the B-17 Flying Fortress was the most-produced variant of the series by Boeing. The B-17G had a Bendix chin turret with twin .50-caliber machine guns to better defend against enemy-fighter frontal attacks, a weakness in previous models. The B-17 lacked the range, bomb load, and speed of the Consolidated B-24 Liberator, but it was preferred by many crews due to its easier flying characteristics, defensive armament, higher service ceiling, and the airplane's ability to make it back to base when heavily damaged, sometimes even with two or more engines damaged.

Source of photo: U.S. Air Force

2-2 Big Yank—B-17G "Big Yank" of the 483rd Bomb Group, 15th Air Force (1945). Note the portrait of President Franklin D. Roosevelt on the nose of the aircraft behind the chin turret. The G model was designed and made by Boeing, but construction of the aircraft was also farmed out to Douglas and Lockheed-Vega to speed production. Source: United States National Archives

2-3 Liberator—The Consolidated B-24J Liberator was the other heavy, four-engine bomber of the Eighth Air Force. The B-24 was produced in greater numbers than any other U.S. bomber. It was used extensively by the Fifteenth Air Force in the Mediterranean Theater, flying from bases in Italy and North Africa, destroying submarines in the Battle of the Atlantic and the Pacific Theater against Japanese forces. It was the first bomber with tricycle landing gear. Its main design feature was a high-aspect "Davis Wing" (named after the design engineer)—giving it great lift and range, but also making it more vulnerable to damage or separation from explosives when attacked by fighters or antiaircraft fire.

Source: United States Air Force photo

2-4 B-24M—A late model B-24 of the Fifteenth Air Force, based in Italy, releasing bombs on enemy railroad yards at Muhldorf, Germany (19 March 1945), near the end of the war. This late variant had a movable machine gun turret mounted in the tail, similar to the nose turret.

Source: United States Air Force

2-5 Rage in Heaven—The B-24J "Rage in Heaven" of the 492nd Bomb Group, North Pickenham Air Station. The wild paint scheme on the wings and fuselage indicates it was a lead formation assembly ship for guiding the bomber formations.

Source: United States Air Force photo

2-6 Mustang—The North American P-51D Mustang, the long-range fighter that enabled the army air force to gain supremacy over the Luftwaffe. The Mustang could escort heavy bomber formations to the farthest reaches of Nazi Germany. The Mustangs pictured here are from the 375th Fighter Squadron, Eighth Air Force. The aircraft's performance was greatly enhanced with the Rolls-Royce Merlin engine. The external fuel tanks extended its range.

Source: United States Air Force photo

2-7 Thunderbolt—The Republic P-47 Thunderbolt was built in greater numbers than any U.S. fighter plane. It was the heaviest single engine fighter in WWII, powered by an eighteen-cylinder R3350 Pratt and Whitney double-row radial engine, producing 2,200 horsepower. The Thunderbolt, or "Jug," also performed as a fighter-bomber, attacking enemy troops, tanks, transportation, and airfields and aircraft. The P-47 was used extensively by the Ninth Air Force, as it moved bases throughout the continent of Europe to support advancing American and other Allied ground forces.

Source: United States Air Force photo

2-8 Lightning—The Lockheed P-38 Lightning was a twin-engine, twin-tail fighter used in all combat theaters. The Lightning had a maximum speed of 414 mph and was powered by two Allison V1710 in-line engines. It could carry four .50-caliber machine guns, a 20-mm cannon, and up to two thousand pounds of bombs and rockets.

Source: U.S. Air Force photo

2-9 Marauders-The twin engine Martin B-26 Marauder was used extensively by the Ninth Tactical Army Air Force in the European Theatre, as the Ninth relocated bases across the continent to support Allied ground forces. The B-26 was a high performance airplane and had to be flown with great care. It unfairly earned a reputation as a "widow maker" in the Training Commands, due to accidents resulting from high takeoff and landing speeds required by its design. These issues were addressed in later models by increased wing span, tail and rudder changes, and, more intensive training. The Marauder developed an excellent safety record, and could withstand a lot of battle damage. The photographs show an interesting close view of the B-26 and crew in flight, and, Women's Air Service Pilots (WASPS) with B-26 Marauders they ferried to Larado, Texas in 1944. The WASPS in this photo seemed very capable of handling the high performance Marauders.

Source: U.S. Air Force photos.

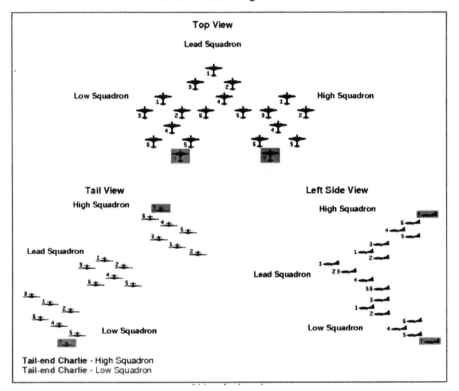

Standard Group Combat Box Formation of 20 Aircraft - August 1943

2-10 Combat Box—This diagram shows in three dimensions the typical combat box formation for aerial defense and bombing accuracy. The combat box was introduced by General Curtis LeMay when he was commander of the 305th Bomb Group in England in 1943.

Source: 303rd Bomb Group Association website

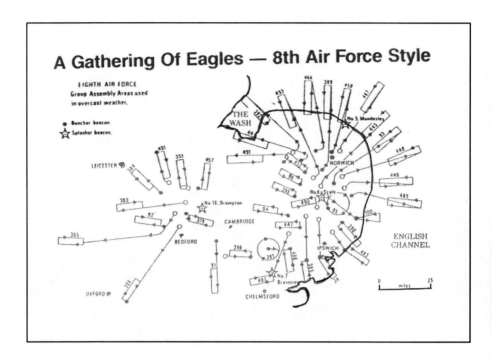

2-11 Gathering of Eagles—The drawing shows the location of "buncher" and "splasher" beacons to guide the assembly of bomber squadron, group, and wing formations after takeoff from bases in east central England. These beacons had a predetermined Morse code signal. After each aircraft took off, it would climb and circle to its assigned altitude given at the mission briefing. A bomber's radio compass would guide it to circle the group's "buncher" beacon. When all squadron and group ships were assembled, they would head east and assemble as part of their respective combat wings around the assigned "splasher" beacon near the English Channel. Once all combat wings had achieved their respective altitudes and positions within the formation then all aircraft could head out on the bombing mission.

Source: U.S. Air Force Archives.

II. THE FIRST FIVE

The first few missions were very important to the mental altitude of a crew. If a crew was badly shot up on an early mission, the experience often left its members at least partially crippled in their mental altitude and nerve condition for the rest of their tour. And if their first missions were short, easy ones, with weak or sparse enemy opposition, they often built up an unspoken, dreaded expectation of that day which they knew was bound to come. On the other hand, if a crew flew to tough targets, where there was a lot of opposition in the form of fighters or flak, or both, and came through unscathed, the fact they survived those first ones gave them great confidence.

In this particular respect, my crew fared well. When we landed at the end of our fifth mission we had logged over forty hours of combat time and had been to Berlin three times and Kiel twice. In those five missions we experienced most of the sights and sensations which were bound to come sooner or later. Although we sustained comparatively little flak damage, we flew through intense flak on each of those missions, and perhaps that fostered the belief which grew on us that we were one of those lucky crews destined to complete their tour of missions. We had seen B-17s explode by flak burst, and we had seen the chutes pop below falling bombers. Fragments of our own formation's planes had whipped past our windows and, on one occasion, an empty parachute—the emptiest, loneliest thing in the world—had floated past our wing. We had seen the cripples falling slowly and inexorably back from the formations, struggling forward, sliding backward, finally giving up in despair and turning desperately homeward, to fight the long battle alone. By what we had seen, we knew what we had missed, and in our inexperience, we began to consider ourselves as seasoned veterans. We knew that we had already hurdled some excellent opportunities to get shot down. We knew that no amount of prior training could teach the many small, inconspicuous, but important things which a crew learned in those first missions by making mistakes. We had made mistakes, had been lucky, and had learned from them.

But on that first morning, 7 May 1944, when the screen rolled up in the briefing rooms and I saw the red line running to Berlin; when I saw the huge blotch of red which represented the flak area, with the target in the middle; especially when I saw my name above number five cross, low squadron, low box, on the formation diagram; when I saw those things I was not so sure about our Divine Destiny. And judging from their expressions, the others of the crew felt the same vague uncertainty. Strangely, the thought occurred to me how ignominious it would be to go down on the first mission. Later on, perhaps not so bad. But now—the very first one—would be definitely humiliating and embarrassing.

My copilot for this mission was Lieutenant Hamilton, a husky blonde fellow from Pennsylvania, who was from one of the seasoned crews of our squadron. We were to know Hamilton and his other crew members well, as the officers lived in the barracks next to us. Jack flew with Walsh, pilot of Hamilton's crew, in this exchange arrangement which was a group policy for new crews on their first mission.

Hamilton was very helpful and tactful and was in every way a fine copilot. Whereas we were at the point where being shot down would have been a humiliating thing, Hamilton, with sixteen missions, stood at the point where it would have been somewhat of a damn shame!

Some vivid impressions remain from that first mission. I remember the droll, puzzled expression on Miller's (engineer) face as he sat in the briefing room and looked at Berlin on the map, with the red line running to it from our base. The situation was so very similar to a morning just over a month ago, when we sat in a briefing room at Dalhart, Texas, and heard the briefing for a routine training flight—similar, and yet so different. No doubt, he was wondering just how the change could have come about so quickly.

True to form for new crews, we needed every minute of the time between briefings and takeoff. When Hamilton, Frank Ricks, and I arrived at the hardstand one hour before takeoff time, the gunners were rushing about the ship lugging .50-caliber machine guns, huge belts of ammunition, and heated suits. We complicated the situation by getting in the way of all of them. There was no time for the pretty little pep talk I had in mind. Instead of gathering for a last-minute huddle, as we were to do in later missions, we scrambled aboard at the last minute like the traditional herd of turtles. Harry Baker stowed his ball turret and scrambled in the rear door just in time to escape the starting blast of number three engine, and Miller rushed out to pick up his Mae West from the hardstand as we started to move out to the perimeter track.

Once we were in the air, we settled down to the normal routine of a mission. Miraculously, nothing had been left on the ground that was essential, and we found our place in formation—on the left wing of Walsh, who led the second element of the low squadron.

Enemy territory. It was strange, this sensation, when—for the first time—you found yourself over an enemy country. There was a certain strain of unbelief and a suggestion of unreality. It was difficult to realize that, in a few minutes of flying time, you had suddenly transferred yourself from a situation where those below you were friends to one where all those below you were enemies. Five minutes ago, you could have peeled out of formation and landed at any one of a dozen fields; friendly voices would have guided you in for a landing, and a bouncing little jeep with a big FOLLOW ME sign on its back would have tolled your big ship in to its place on the ramp. Five minutes ago, people below you were tracking you on strange electronic devices, and their purpose was to aid you and direct you, if necessary, on your way. Now those below were tracking too, but with deadly intent. They sought to destroy you, for they were deathly afraid of you. If you left formation now, you were marked for doom. Instead of friendly voices, the fields below would send up deadly AA fire or fighter planes. A few minutes ago, you could have landed anywhere below you and been back to your base the next day; now, if you got on the ground at all, you would be a prisoner in enemy hands for an indefinite period—perhaps for years. That was the best that could happen to you if you were forced to leave this formation now. It was a rather startling realization.

Flak bursts, too, registered strangely on this first mission. Up ahead, as we turned on the bomb run, was an aerial skeletonized outline of the city of Berlin above a solid cloud deck. Here above the clouds, we could see no glimpse of the city below; yet even with our line of flight, above and below, were hundreds of flak bursts.

The thought came to me, "Why, this is even worse than they said it was." The old bursts were merging into a pall of gray smoke, and new ones flecked the cloud with black splashes. Ahead of our formation, and to either side, other wing formations moved though the vast forest of bursts, each going to its special target. While I wondered, fleetingly, how the formations ever got through, the focus on the picture sharpened and we found ourselves moving though this solid, three dimensional structure of flak. The close bursts were so black that there was a sheen on them. They rippled quickly out into varied, irregular patterns, stopped and slowly dissolved. They appeared to be harmless phenomena and to have no substance. It was almost hard to connect these empty puffs with the crippled planes floating below, some trailing smoke, others releasing behind them tiny parachute bubbles; most especially to connect them with that plane just ahead which suddenly disintegrated into several ragged pieces and whipped out of sight.

Hamilton considered himself something in the nature of a guide while we were on the bomb run and immediately after. Having been to Berlin before, he called out things of interest to the gunners on interphone. Only occasional glimpses of the ground could now be had, but he talked about the flak, pointing out where some batteries were evidently firing on the window of tinfoil which was being thrown out by each formation, and calling off the caliber gun which had fired certain bursts. His voice sounded cool and almost nonchalant, and strongly impressed us all.

Formation flying in heavy bombers was a physical task which could be Herculean labor, or a series of easy, effortless reactions, depending upon the experience of the pilot. The average pilot made terrific work out his first few missions and gradually progressed to the more easy and skillful technique as his reflexes were conditioned by experience. Almost invariably the inexperienced pilot did more physical work and got less results; as his experience increased, he did less work and flew better formation. Good formation flying was a science of anticipation, of shrewd judgment of distances and relative speeds, of self control and alert relaxation; and it was a science which could be learned only through long hours at the controls.

On the long route home from Berlin, I learned how much actual physical work was involved in flying formation nine long hours, even rotating the flying between pilot and copilot. I had flown the ship on most of the route in and to the target, despite Hamilton's repeated offers to relieve me. I was 'eager', as we say, and wanted to check myself out thoroughly on this combat formation flying. I tucked our ship in close and felt rather pleased with myself. I was buoyed up by the tension and excitement of this first mission and the thought of getting tired did not enter my mind until after the bomb run. Then on the way home, which was always a time of terrific let-down for the crews unless they were actually under attack, my arms and legs became lead. My flying, which had been good, became extremely sloppy. I could not anticipate the relative movements of my own ship and its lead, and I began to jockey the throttles back and forth excessively and to tug and heave on the controls more than was necessary. In short, I began to do some very ragged and poor flying, all because I was bone tired from a kind of exertion which was entirely new to me. The result was that by the time we landed Hamilton had done his full share of flying.

When we landed, we discovered to our consternation and—I must say now—delight that our ship had collected quite a number of ragged flak holes, and in the most unexpected places, although there had been no major damage. James Baker crawled out of the fuselage and gazed in fascination at a hole the size of his fist in the tail, just above where his head ordinarily would be. Mussetter examined with great interest a hole in the fuselage just behind the radio operator's table where he sat. Brown and Ricks gaped at several ragged holes in the nose compartment. Even Hamilton and I had something to think about, for we had a couple of holes in the pilots' compartment. Everybody went around and appropriately admired the other fellow's damage, but each one went back for another fascinated look at his own particular flak hole. Later on, they would not be of such morbid interest, and anything less than a feathered prop would not warrant more than a second glance. But for a long time, flak holes were beads on a rosary.

I think the first mission left one feeling somewhat like a punch-drunk fighter at the end of the battle who had fully expected to get a beating, and did, and was amazed and elated to find himself still on his feet at the gong. "I did it," he thought. "I lasted." In a slightly different way, there was this feel of befogged elation. You realized that you had come through a great and strange and unusual experience. Whether you died tomorrow or lived to be a hundred, this was something out of the ken of normal living. I remember with what secret elation I wrote Dad after about three missions: "I haven't been under fire yet, Dad. But I've been over fire, and I think it adds up to the same thing."

Our second mission to Berlin came the following day and caught us before we had recovered from the first one. Before we were aware of it, we had been twice to Berlin and were still living. In almost every way, it was a repetition of the first mission, except that I had Jack as copilot and there were no strangers aboard, and that we were much better organized on the second attempt.

We had a rather long layoff then, due to a streak of bad weather, during which time there were several scrubbed missions. During this period, we learned that scrubbed missions constituted one of the aggravations of combat flying.

On the whole, they were a great nuisance. We qualify this because it would be wrong to say that sometimes the scrubbing of a mission was not welcome. In periods of bad weather, we could always expect that a few missions could be scrubbed. During all of 1944, the Eighth Air Force was a vast machine which operated as regularly and consistently as a well-organized factory. It had the men and the machines (some three thousand bombers and three thousand—plus combat crews) to keep up a continuous day-by-day schedule of destruction, and only the weather interrupted the schedule. And in the latter half of the year, even the weather was minimized as a deterrent factor because of the use of radar blind bombing (Mickey).* It was only when conditions were predicted by weather reconnaissance to be such that formations could not be maintained that missions were called off. Weather reconnaissance was done on the early morning of the missions, and while it was being made, the combat crews of the Eighth and Ninth Air Forces all over England had their briefings and went through the usual pre-mission preparations. If the weather proved to be acceptable, the mission went off as planned; and if not, the mission was scrubbed.

The effect of the scrubbing depended somewhat upon just when it came in the preparations. If the mission was scrubbed (by scrambler telephone) during briefing or just after, and before the crews had gone out to their planes, everybody was pretty well satisfied. Even if it had not promised to be an easy mission, the thought of rudely interrupted sleep was not entirely pushed into the background, yet the idea was very easily revived. It was very easy to give a philosophical shrug and head for the barracks and the sack, stopping en route for another mug of coffee. And never could the simple pleasure of sleep be more fully appreciated than by one who dug

---

*   "Mickey," (H2S and later H2X) was a cloud-penetrating radar system in the airplane that could portray the outline image of land features or man-made structures.

into his bunk at such a time, realizing that the alternative to this would have been his place in a plane heading out to Germany.

But if the mission was scrubbed after the crews were at the hardstands or—as was sometimes the case—after the ships had begun to taxi out for takeoff, the reaction was definite disappointment. No matter what kind of mission had been in store, most men would have preferred to go on rather than to turn back to base. By this time, sleep was a thing long since forgotten, and nervous systems had been keyed to the mission. We are told that in the early days of the Eighth, the matter of scrubbed missions was a very serious morale problem, for in those days, blind bombing was in the experimental and planning stage, and missions were more frequently cancelled because of weather. However, during our tour of combat, the scale of bombing missions was so regular and intense that a few cancelled missions did not cause any morale problems. There was a lot of griping against cruel fate and all that, but often it came from men who already had visions of the sack and a chance to catch up on sleep lost on other missions within the week.

*   *   *

Because formation flying was so important to a mission and so difficult to the newcomer, pilots and copilots probably had more to learn than any of the others in those first days of combat flying. There was a lot more involved than keeping a ship in its place quickly and efficiently and was sometimes a problem in itself, especially to new pilots.

The procedure for rendezvous and assembly of the various combat box and wing formations was essentially very simple. But when bad weather necessitated the changing of briefed altitudes of assembly for the formations, things sometimes became difficult, especially for new crews, who were apt to be more engrossed in affairs in their own ship and to miss some of the VHF announcements of change of altitude.

In the pre-mission briefing, instructions for the assembly were passed out. Each combat box was given a specific altitude of assembly over a certain radio "buncher" or "splasher" ground station, a code name for the leader to use over VHF for identification, and a certain flare combination (lead box, green; high box, red yellow; low box, red, green; etc.) to be fired at regular intervals by the box lead ships. The combat box leaders were the first ships to take off from each group field and they immediately climbed to their proper altitude over the assigned radio splasher where they circled and fired flares at regular intervals. Other ships took off in turn at forty-five-second intervals and climbed to the altitude and place assigned their combat box for rendezvous. All ships climbed at the standard airspeed of 150 mph and rate of climb of 300-400 ft/min on prescribed headings, in order that no ship would overrun the preceding plane, for often formations climbed as individual ships through several thousand feet of solid clouds to a normal formation rendezvous on top of the deck.

The navigator of each plane tuned his radio compass to the designated buncher or splasher frequency and checked for the proper code identification as it came regularly through his earphones. The pilot then simply turned his ship until the radio compass needle was pointed to zero. When a plane passed over the station to which the compass was turned, the needle slowly turned 180 degrees and pointed to the tail of the ship. Thereafter, the ship could circle this particular spot of ground as long as necessary, above a solid overcast, or still climbing, tethered by the slowly revolving radio compass needle. As each individual ship broke out of the cloud layer at or near the proper altitude and point of assembly, all eyes were on the watch for the sparkle of a flare which would be from the lead ship. If things were normal a tiny blob would soon appear ahead or to the side and a flare would flash out, identifying the dot as the lead ship of the box. The wing ships and squadron leads would pop out of the clouds in turn and the formation would gradually take shape as the lead ship continued to make his wide circuit of the assembly area.

This would be going on simultaneously on three different levels—for high, lead, and low boxes of each wing—above each radio assembly point and at many different points all over England. Normally, the altitude spacing between the boxes of each wing formation was one thousand feet, which was ample to eliminate any confusion on the part of a pilot as to which cluster of ships he should join when he came out on the top of the clouds and, more important, was sufficient to prevent combat boxes from crowding or overrunning each other.

But weather can complicate any situation in flying. Wing leaders were then forced to announce changes in assembly altitudes of their several boxes and, as previously mentioned, these announcements were inevitably missed by some of the ships. The result was that on any morning of bad weather, or weather which was not predicted for the assembly areas, there were always some ships flubbing around in the clouds, poking from one formation to another in search of their proper places, and usually bleating over VHF like proverbial lost sheep.

A further complication, not encountered in good weather, was the natural tendency of formation leaders to crib just a few hundred feet or so on the other fellow's altitude if, by doing so, they could drag their own formation out of the clouds. This was all right unless the clouds were in layers, as they sometimes were, and close together—in which case we had the unhappy situation of two boxes cribbing altitude in opposite directions, which meant that they would almost meet in the middle. This was rather uncomfortable for the high and low squadrons concerned.

It was on such mornings that boxes or wings were apt to execute the unconventional and hazardous movement known as "shuffling the deck," in which movement two or more boxes inadvertently ran together, resulting in a wild scramble of planes. Even under the best conditions, the airspace over England was unbelievably crowded during the assembly of heavy bomber formations for the day's work. This was especially true during most of 1944 and to the end of the war, for during this period, the Eighth Air Force put up many maximum-effort missions. Unless every formation moved exactly where it was supposed to move, when it supposed to move, there was bound to be some congestion.

Jack and I learned about this on our third mission, which was to Kiel, and we also learned that prop wash from a combat box of B-17s had all the force of a tidal wave. We had just found our place in formation and had tucked our ship into the proper slot with all the satisfaction of young puppies learning new tricks, when our box ran afoul of another group of planes, which came in at an angle and caught the box leader by surprise. Since a formation of twelve or eighteen big airplanes is a rather unwieldy mass that simply cannot be jerked about randomly, the leader had no choice but to bore right through the prop wash of the other group, which managed to turn off just in front of him. Perhaps the older pilots anticipated this and managed to steady themselves a little—though not to escape a severe buffeting—for the more experienced hands usually kept an eye out for this sort of thing. But we, being new, were so intent upon the job of formation flying that neither of us saw or anticipated what was about to happen. Prop wash from the overrun group struck us like a wall of water. The ship rocked and tossed like a chip in a millrace, and we were over on a wingtip several times before we were free of the prop wash. The formation had momentarily opened, up and we felt better to see that other ships had been thrown about also. But when we regained our place, Jack and I were wiser by one experience. Many times afterward, we battled prop wash, but never so helplessly as this first time. Later, we learned to see it coming, to gauge when it would strike, and to ease on power and steady the ship in time.

*   *   *

Luck was a word used often and loosely in combat. Men fell into the habit of speaking in terms of luck—of saying that on such and such an occasion they were lucky, or that their unlucky number did not appear on a certain mission. In its various connotations, we used the word to explain happenings which were the result of curious combinations of circumstances: the fruits of individual skill, diligence, prudence, or lack of any or all or dispensations of Divine Providence. It was in this latter sense, however, that it was most frequently used. What we were trying to rationalize was not that some men lived and others died, but that, as it seems, some men were sought out by Death and others were passed over under particularly deadly circumstances.

Any crew that finished a tour of missions could look back on certain occasions when, by all rights and reason, they could have been collectively dead. Others just as strong, just as intelligent, and just as imbued with a spirit of high living, just as much potential to the future of the world had, under similar circumstances, vanished in a puff of smoke and the dull thud of an explosion.

Our first try at the fourth mission was scrubbed after formations were well on the way to the target. Clouds and contrails had proved impossible, the fighter escort had not been able to get off the ground, and our formations returned to base with full bomb loads after an hour over enemy territory. The flare paths had been lighted in the semidarkness at home fields, and formations slung low in the murky visibility for the standard close approach. We were flying as the number three ship in the low squadron, lead box, that day. Our squadron leader peeled off at the proper time, and we followed him around in turn. The lead ship drifted and sank ahead of us on his approach to the landing runway, and we followed the flare path in. We were settling our heavy ship in for a better-than-my-average landing when I see red flares—the signal to go around—springing up at the edge of the runway, right in front of our ship. It was too late! We were on the runway, and we throttled and braked quickly to taxi speed. The flares continued to go up, and the next ship thundered low overhead in a go-around. In the murk ahead, we saw a vague shape, which developed rapidly into a B-17 sitting athwart the runway a scant halfway down the length of it. Jack unlocked the tail wheel and we skidded by her, inches (not yards) between our wing and the body of our lead ship.

Later, we learned what had happened and knew how narrowly our ships had escaped collision. Our squadron leader had inadvertently landed with his brakes locked. As the heavy ship struck the runway, landing-gear tires had burst, and the ship came to a stop approximately halfway down. In the meantime, our plane had been careening in close behind it, in the correct procedure for a close approach under conditions of poor visibility.

Only good timing and exact landing on the part of both ships had averted a tragedy. The pilot of the lead plane landed well down the runway, in order to give ample clearance to the ships following him. This was proper, though not always so exactly done as in this case. And we, as the second ship to land, had come in for a smooth landing close behind him. Our only error had been in landing so near the edge of the runway as second ship, and this was a very fortunate error. The red flares, which registered on us too late for a go-around, warned us of trouble, so that Jack and I were able to bring the ship to a near stop and to turn off the runway as we approached the crippled ship ahead.

Not always had we made our near-perfect landings. Not always had we been able to stop at the first intersection. Sometimes we, as most others, lurched to a two-bounce landing well down the runway and smoked brakes to a stop at the very end. But this particular time, under these lethal circumstances, we had come in perfectly. Any other way could have been a disaster.

CHAPTER THREE

COMBAT CREW

3-1 Combat Crew: James F. "Jimmy" Risher, Jack Refining, Frank Ricks, Vincent "VE" Brown. Standing: Jennings Miller, Rudy Croce, "Moose" Mussetter, Harry Baker, Bob Ockerman, James Baker. Photo may have been taken at the Dalhart, Texas, army airfield.

Courtesy 401st Bomb Group Association.

III. Combat Crew

The heavy bomber crew was one of the many small units of men which were the basic elements of all our military forces. The past war (WWII) has at various times been called "the war of supply," "the war of distances and transport," "the war of logistics," and "the war of airpower/sea power" in attempts to emphasize one or another important phase of military efforts. It was, of course, a war of all descriptions and much more. We prefer to think of it as "the war of small teams," based on the fact that all conflict hinged on the actions of small cohesive units of men operating as separate entities in total forces engaged. On the ground and in the air, as well as on and under the sea, men were parceled out in small groups to service and operate the machines of war. Tank crews, artillery gun crews, rifle squads, PT boat crews, AA gun crews, and air combat crews—these and others were the backbone and the substance of all our combat forces. All men who saw combat had for their first loyalty to that team, whatever it was, of which they were a part.

The size of the groups or teams and the types of specialists composing them were dependent upon the size and complexity of the machines and the nature of their employment. The composition of the Flying Fortress crew was based on this machine's design and use as a heavily defended platform for the transport of bombs and their delivery to enemy targets. The functions of the machine were threefold: precise, controlled movement to a destination and return to point of origin; accurate delivery of bombs on a designated target; and active self-defense against all attacking forces opposing its mission. The two pilots, the radio operator, and the navigator were necessary to the operation of the machine and its proper navigation to and from the target. The bombardier was necessary to the operation of equipment involved in actually dropping or delivering the bombs. The five gunners were necessary to the proper aiming and firing of the thirteen .50-caliber machine guns, installed in four turrets and three other gun positions as a defense of the machine and its occupants against enemy attacks. There was some overlap of duties. One of the waist gun positions was manned by the aerialing engineer who was important to the overall operation of the aircraft; bombardier fired the chin turret, and radio manned a single .50-caliber gun.

This was the factual basis upon which ten men were assembled as a bomber crew. These men, four officers and six enlisted men, were dependent upon each other for their very lives. Each time they flew a mission, they were drawn closer together in a unique bond of comradeship. Each return from a mission increased their total of mutual accomplishments and their interdependence.

Naturally enough, with men so closely associated, the rubbing of individual personalities one against the other was all-important. The fortunate truth is, of course, that almost any assortment of ten normal Americans was a workable combination, given time and common experience to draw the men together. But it was also true that sometimes individuals found they simply could not get along with a certain crew of men; or two or more men felt such constant friction between them that they knew they could never stay on the same crew with any harmony.

The possibility of incurable clashes of personality was well recognized in the Training Command, and every effort was made to effect substitutions or changes before a crew ever finished training and headed for combat. The pilot, as commander of the crew, was responsible for discovering and bringing to light any chronic friction between members of his crew and, if it should be necessary, secure changes in crew members for the good of all members concerned. Thus, most crews had—when they appeared in the combat air force—long since found themselves harmonious combinations, or had found clashes and remedied them by changes.

While this was worth mentioning as an index of how closely these few men lived, it could easily be exaggerated. There really were not many such clashes. For the most part, the surviving combat crews had the same rosters at the end of their missions as they had at the beginning of their training.

Rank on a combat crew was as much a badge of technical skill or rating as a delineation of authority. True, the pilot was the crew and airplane commander, and if the crew was a good one, he was the commander in fact as well as name. Yet the good pilot and successful crew commander usually commanded simply by being a skillful and capable pilot and a reasonably well-rounded personality, considerate of his crew and genuinely interest in their welfare. To men who depended upon his flying skill for their lives, nothing else was as important, and nothing could take the place of it. The same was true of all other positions on a crew. The radio operator who knew his radio was apt to be respected and valued by his crew; the navigator who knew his job; and the gunners who were alert and capable with their turrets. Nothing could be more important to all men of a crew than that each man knew his job and did it well. Thus, it was that each mission flown added to the confidence and unspoken loyalty of a crew. Each mission told them that they were good and that they could work together as an effective team.

Our crew, I believe, was fairly typical of the hundreds which were assembled, trained, and fed into the crucible of war. If there was any exception to the norm, it was, perhaps, in the crew commander. I was somewhat older than the average when at twenty-seven years and two months, I received my wings at Ellington Field, Houston, Texas, in July 1943. I was twenty-eight years old when I flew our second mission on 8 May 1944 (the first on May 7). I probably was at least five years older than the average pilot in our combat formations during our tour of combat. Four years of college (The Citadel, Charleston, South Carolina), a year of teaching and one of graduate study, and over a year of infantry active duty as a junior officer preceding Air Corps experience.

This background could well have caused me to be reserved and perhaps more militant than the average crew commander in my initial relations with my crew. But my gut recollection of the whole experience is that we all came to respect each other and our total worth as a crew before we departed Dalhart Air Base, Texas, in early March 1944 flying a brand new B-17 on our way to combat. As our training missions had progressed, we had come to know each other, and the total personality of our crew had begun to develop. I felt that I knew the other members of the crew pretty well by this time.

Jack Refenning, our copilot (from Ohio), was Irish, effervescent, lively, and alert. His temper and his humor were equally in evidence and, generally, in excellent balance. Jack was a born fighter pilot, but he happened to be one of those single-engine graduates who—because of the needs of the moment—were drafted into the job of flying copilot on the heavies, rather than going on to the fighters they had dreamed of flying. Only a pilot could understand what a disappointment he and the others like him had to overcome. Jack was generally more on the surface with his feeling and reactions than I was; yet we had a common characteristic, and that was our intenseness on the job when we were in the cockpit. I sometimes thought it was no small marvel that he and I, considering our respective temperaments, were able to fly an airplane together through a tour of missions without some sort of clash. The wonder was that, with our high-strung dispositions, we managed to counterbalance each other's moods during many days when even the best tempers were short.

Brown (VE) our bombardier, was nonchalant and slightly cynical in attitude. He was utterly frank toward life and had a fine dry humor which made him the author of many of our pet bywords and phrases. If he thought, for example, that someone was unduly impressed with his own importance, VE was apt to state blandly that he too "used to wrack balls in pool halls." VE was from Precklis Neglis, a mythical town in Arizona, the location of which was still very vague. He was a ready man for gin and/or Guinness or any other reasonable vintage with good company. He was somewhat uneager, as the expression went in the Air Corps, in his attitude toward routine things. He concentrated on his work in the air or his preparation for a mission, but he was not zealous toward the regular ground duties.

Frank Ricks, navigator (from California), was our "fair-headed boy." Frank was a bashfully good-looking young man. He was reserved, extremely intelligent, quietly efficient. Because of his naiveté—which was, I am convinced, his particular form of humor—he was the object of much kidding.

McClung (Mac), who replaced him, was in many ways an opposite number. "Mac" was a big, hearty, loquacious Texan. He had a ready laugh, a bluff humor, and a great capacity for enjoying life. Mac instantly achieved a natural and easy personal relationship with each and all.

Mussetter (Moose), our radio operator, was tempestuous—somewhat unpredictable in moods. His smile and his scowl were always chasing each other. It was not surprising that the Moose reacted violently to the new stress of combat missions and that he, at first, showed signs of wear under the strain. He complained, after the first few missions, that he could not sleep, that the men in the barracks made too much noise in the evenings. In those first days over Berlin, Kiel, and other targets, the flak-infested bomb runs tested him. We finally discovered that Moose suffered from claustrophobia in the confines of the radio compartment, most especially on the bomb runs. This compartment gave very limited outside view—less than any other crew position. The Moose knew there was flak out there, but he couldn't see it, and this stressed him. We tried letting him come up and stand between the pilot and the copilot seats on the bomb run (there was nothing he could do back there on the bomb run), and this worked strangely well. I always thought that a simple swap of positions between Moose and I on the bomb run would have been preferable, had it been possible. At any rate, this solved the problem. During the latter half of our mission, the Moose hung over the open bomb bays as soon as the bombs were dropped and was the first to give forth on interphone about the bomb strike.

Jennings Miller, engineer (from Illinois), was quiet, soft-spoken, inscrutable. He was slow, deliberate, and methodical to the extreme. He had an inquisitive mind and a penchant for gathering odd bits of information. He spent much of his free time in the combat crew library, culling over intelligence reports and bulletins and reading the various magazines and papers there. He was in every way a steady and reliable person and a stalwart member of our crew.

Rudolph (Rudy) Groce, our left waist gunner (from New York), was an intense boy with a half-hidden reservoir of personality. He and Mussetter were solid pals and spent much of their leave time together. Groce was a quiet but positive partner in their many excursions.

Harry Baker, ball turret gunner (from Kansas), was open, frank, extremely diligent, and conscientious—persistent in all things. He was inventive, inquisitive, and resourceful. If any of us wanted an article which we thought was not to be had, we went to Harry Baker, and he often produced it. Harry was also a very religious person and soon earned the respected title of Parson Baker.

James Baker (no relation to Harry) from Minnesota was a quiet and reserved young man who thought much more than he talked. He was the type of man whom people learn quickly to depend upon, without question or doubt. As a tail gunner, he rode in a lonely, isolated spot. His spot furnished the most severe test of an aerodynamic stomach, for the tail of a B-17 in close formation was somewhat like the end of a whip: the slightest movement of the whole body was accentuated and increased violently there. I shudder to think how many times James had cause to silently curse Jack and me in his lonely habitat.

Robert (Bob) Ockerman, our top turret gunner and armorer (from Iowa), was a hale and hearty extrovert and a well-balanced young man. Somehow he typified "young America at war" to me, for he did so definitely look upon this thing as a trial that must be endured, and so eagerly looked to home, wife, and the plains of Iowa as the ultimate and only worthy end.

It was somewhere along between the fifth and tenth missions that combat crews began to come out of the initial daze and adjust their perspectives to this unusual life. Perhaps the most significant element of change was the development of a subtle and unspoken bond, which welded the individuals of a crew into one crew personality. This bond, in its higher degree, came only through association and cooperation in long hours of common danger. It existed to a certain extent on the normal crew when they flew the first mission, and it was compounded with each mission followed. It was evident chiefly in that clannish spirit which caused all men to dislike flying with a crew other than their own. Not only had each crew worked out its own system of operation on missions and established countless little procedures—known more formerly as standard operating procedures in larger units—but each member of the crew had gradually developed a feeling that he would function better and more securely with its members, and was irreplaceable.

This fact was brought home to my crew when our squadron operations officer informed me, between our fifth and sixth missions, that Frank Ricks would be reassigned to another crew as navigator.

An older crew—which did not, at the time, have a navigator—was being groomed as a lead, and Ricks was the most promising new navigator for the lead crew assignment. I was told that we would have assigned to us the next new navigator who joined the squadron. This was logical and a necessary move, and I recognized it as such; but for me and the rest of the crew at the time, it was like a death in the family. We felt crippled and lost and doomed. We could not at the time visualize flying the long procession of combat missions with anybody but Frank Ricks crouched over the navigator's table. We felt that our combat tour, whatever its outcome, had already been turned into a calamity.

Undoubtedly, the low point of our morale as a crew was that period of some ten days between the time Frank Ricks was removed from our crew and Guy McClung ("Mac") was assigned and flew his first mission with us. Mac sold us to a man on his first mission, and the gap was filled to the satisfaction of all. But so far as our feelings were concerned, we—in effect—had two navigators, and the fact that Ricks flew with another crew simply gave us another plane and crew to worry about on missions.

*   *   *

We were a harmonious crew, and personal clashes and differences were at a minimum. It would be too much to expect that men engaged in this kind of business would always be unctuous and soft-spoken to each other, but with us at least, any occasional friction or differences were passing instances. In most cases where one individual was irritated or angry about something, the situation was such that the rest of us got more than enough amusement out of it to compensate for his anger or discomfiture.

Typical of this was a little exchange between VE and Mussetter (Moose) one afternoon on a practice bombing mission.

VE was dropping practice bombs on the old hulk in the water at Brest Sands peninsula (bomb range) and Mussetter was spotting his strikes from the open bomb bay. We were dropping from low altitudes (three thousand feet) and flying a "clover leaf pattern," dropping a bomb each time we came around over the target ship—as regular and unspectacular as a man plowing his field. VE was in the groove that afternoon and had racked up three shacks (bull's eye hit) and five close strikes in the water as we came around for the last one.

"Watch this one close, Moose," he called as we neared the time of bomb release. We continued the run, the ship making slight, weaving turns as his last corrections on the bomb sight reacted to autopilot.

"Bombs away," he sang, and no doubt leaned back from the sight, waiting confidently for Mussetter to the call shack. Seconds passed and he inquired anxiously, and a little impatiently, "What about it, Moose?"

"Oh, there it is now," called the Moose nonchalantly after a pause. "Ah-h-h-h about four hundred feet at six o'clock."

Jack and I, stirred from the monotony of tending the autopilot, grinned and waited.

"Damit to hell! bellowed VE on the interphone. "I don't see how that can be. Either the sight's screwy or somebody can't see back there, and the sight's been dropping them all right."

We chuckled as he continued his tirade, piling up evidence that somebody couldn't see back there.

"All right, all right, so I'm blind!" the Moose replied. "So you better spot your own bombs." And in righteous indignation, this son of Massachusetts retired behind his funny book in the radio room as we hurtled low over the English countryside on our way to home base.

CHAPTER FOUR

D-DAY AND AFTER

4-1 D-Day—Paratroopers prepare to board a C-47 Skytrain, to parachute into Normandy in advance of the invasion beach assaults by Allied Armies at Omaha, Utah, Sword, and Juno Beaches. The white stripes on the C-47 were an Allied recognition symbol for D-Day air operations.

Source of photo: National Archives

4-2 Paratroopers—U.S. paratroopers proudly display items captured during combat with German troops, D-Day plus two.

Source: National Archives photo

401st COMMANDING OFFICER LEADS 1500 HEAVY BOMBERS ON MISSION OVER LE BOURGET

The privilege of leading the greatest force of heavy bombers ever assembled in one unit in the history of aerial warfare was that of Col. Harold W. Bowman, Commanding Officer of the 401st Bombardment Group.

The mission was performed a few days after "D-Day" and the target was world-famous Le Bourget airdrome at Paris, up until the day of the mission used as a fighter and bomber base by the German Air Force.

"It simply was a story of good navigation," Col. Bowman said. "We clicked right to the initial point using dead reckoning and pilotage. On the run in, visibility was bad, but my bombardier found the target and we smacked the hell out of it."

The Colonel admits he was pleased to have the honor of leading this record-breaking number of bombers, but he is more pleased with the bombing results, which officially are scored as "excellent."

It was the first visual bombing of Col. Bowman's force since D-Day and en route to the target crewmen craned their necks to see what they could of the French Invasion coast. Activity was intense, smoke could be seen coming from Bayeaux and Caen.

Pilot of Col. Bowman's aircraft was Capt. James F. Goodman; Major Julius Pickoff was bombardier; Captain James F. Egan and Capt. Walter E. Haberer, navigators.

CAPT. HABERER, MAJ. PICKOFF, COL. BOWMAN

The "OK" sign is given by Col. Harold W. Bowman, right, on the biggest mission yet flown by the Eighth Air Force over occupied Europe, to his bombardier, Major Julius Pickoff, and his navigator, Capt. Walter E. Haberer, on their return to home base.

Captain Jim Goodman piloted the lead aircraft on the mission to Le Bourget Airdrome near Paris which led the First Division's biggest effort to date. The target was plastered and the attacking force was by far the largest ever sent out of England

4-3 The 401st on D-Day—These pictures and story are from the Pictorial Record Album of the 401st Bomb Group, published in 1948. The "Mighty Eighth" launched over 1,600 bombers to support the Allied invading forces on the Normandy Beaches on D-Day. The 401st led the mission, bombing German Air Force installations to keep the Luftwaffe quiet for the invasion. By the D-Day Invasion, the U. S. Strategic Air Forces and Tactical Air Forces had gained dominance over the skies over Europe.

Source: 401st Bomb Group Pictorial Record Album (1948)

IV. D-DAY AND AFTER

D-Day came as a sudden clap of thunder to the heavy bomber forces, as it did to the rest of the world, even though we had signs and portents of coming events. There had been a charged stillness in the air, as before a violent thunderstorm on a hot summer afternoon. Even from the situation of the bomber bases, on the northern and outer rim of the composite military installation which was Southern England, some implication of the great furious preparations which were going on along the coastal belt could be felt. There on the crescent of bases north of London, something of the atmosphere of tense and active waiting pervaded, although the work of the heavy bombers went on as usual. We felt the pressure of a terrible force which was building slowly to a point of inevitably explosion. But we knew only that invasion was coming sometime, and that great forces were assembled and waiting.

Armies and tactical air commands were being welded together in last minute training and final beach assault rehearsals were being conducted; fleets of landing craft and supply vessels were being assembled for loading, and mountainous stockpiles of supplies and equipment grew along the wharves. Military camps were so thick in South England that space for maneuvers and exercises was a problem. While this stupendous training and logistical effort, too large for any one mind to understand or encompass completely, swelled and developed to its inevitable climax, the specialized phase of attack by heavy bombers, which was a prerequisite to the greater effort building up, continued and increased in intensity.

Late in the afternoon of May, in the semidarkness, long beaded snakes of C-47s towing gliders wound over the countryside in final maneuvers. On our bases, sidearms were issued (but no ammunition) and warnings against enemy sabotage attempts were repeatedly made. Base defense units increased the frequency of their nightly defense exercise and, for the first time, a tense, and militant undercurrent was experienced on bomber bases, which were normally as peaceful in atmosphere as any military installations. London, when we visited it on pass, was strangely deserted of military personnel, by comparison with its former over run state. Only Air Corps—largely from the bomber bases—were to be seen, except for the usual headquarters personnel.

And yet in our group it was a surprise to all who rose for an early morning mission on 6 June when at the beginning of briefing Colonel Bowman announced that "This is the day." Those words were sufficient to tell the story and, for the first and only time that I can recall, there was a loud and outspoken sentiment and fervor. For fully five minutes the briefing room was a hubbub of noise and cheering. For once, implications, at least, of a secret leaked out of the briefing room, if anyone outside had thought to connect the cheering with what prompted it. No doubt there were men who that morning for the first, and possibly last time, were completely enthusiastic and glad of an event which held only danger and possible death for them; who sensed that they were living and participating in one of the greatest moments of history, even thought they could not comprehend it in full.

Our mission that morning was directly connected with the Invasion operations, though it was not a "close support" mission. The wing targets were German airdrome installations in Nothern France. The entire Eighth Air Force operated in the area of Northern France that morning, for the purpose of quelling enemy airpower in that area and disrupting enemy movements in the rear areas. Thus, on this day and for a considerable number of days in the next month, the Eighth Air Force threw its weight into Northern France with the Ninth Tactical Air Force, varying in its strategic bombing with semi-tactical bombing to further the ground forces in their campaign.

I had always found time, after the first few missions, to relax mentally for a few minutes after my craft was in place in the formation and while we were making the last wide circuits of the assembly area. For those few minutes I could sit there feeling as relaxed as I ever have in a rocking chair. And each time this query would strike me as if it were a new and original thought: Where are you now and what are you doing here? Why are you here suspended in space, at a point which can be identified only by an intangible radio wave; in this machine which was made, not by one man, but by thousands, and which does not belong to you or any of these men aboard it, or to any one person who can be named? The question, as it came to me, did not involve issues of the war or of its right or wrong aspects. Rather, it was a query which has occurred to me many times in other places, and must have to others also, involving the eternal riddle of separate human destinies. It was a question without any definite answer that I know but its implications were as tantalizing as conjecture on the limits of space.

And on that morning of 6 June 1944 as our formation headed out to the English coast over a solid blanket of clouds, it was more tantalizing than ever. How was it that each man of the million and more involved in the colossal undertaking came to his specific place, in a landing craft; in the engine room of a destroyer; on the bridge of a cruiser; a member of the underground in France, carrying on the long struggle for months before this day; pilot of a fighter plane or engineer of a bomber; commander of a regiment or of an army? Yet it mattered not so much, even if there had been an answer, as the fact that each and all, from the highest to lowest, was a chip in the millrace of destiny. However his individual qualifications or endeavors had changed or would change his relative place, each individual rode as a helpless particle on this irresistible movement of collective human force. No man in all this multitude was free, except his inmost soul. This was a torrent of force, and its waters were drawn from all the world. It transcended and overpowered all that could be associated with individual identity. It was only in the continuity of this thing that the individual mattered; only that thousands upon thousands of human particles still in the quiet backstretches of the stream would be inexorably drawn to the vortex, and that individual success or failure, greatness or weakness, in any and all places, would affect the indrawn stream in countless ways that could not be predicted or measured.

I, for one, could not frame the suggestions of mighty human drama unfolding on the earth and knew only that I was privileged to be less than a millionth part of the greatest organization of human effort ever assembled for one purpose: that I had power in my hands, and my purpose was right; that our formation was moving out on the pinnacle of a stupendous three-dimensional human enterprise more complicated, intricate, and involved than anything the world has ever seen before, or would again.

And yet the curtain was drawn below us, and we saw nothing of what went on beneath. This D-Day mission was easier than most of our missions. Cloud cover was heavy over the channel and over the target area. Flak was light, and enemy aircraft were nowhere to be seen above the cloud layer. Friendly fighters of all descriptions popped in and out of the clouds and gave teasing evidence that something was happening below. When formations returned to base, the first question was as to whether or not the invasion had gone off as planned.

*   *   *

The invasion of the continent affected the heavy bomber operations in several ways: chiefly, perhaps, in that the whole scale of operations was increased. The day by day pounding of German targets went on as usual but some of the effort of the Eighth Air Force was concentrated on targets in France. These missions were of varying lengths, but shorter than most of the missions in Germany. A mission of four or five hours was—to us—comparatively short, and this was the general average of the trips to France. Whereas the missions were shorter, they came more often, and the month of June and much of July passed in a blur for combat crews.

From 7 June to 7 July, my crew flew fifteen missions (or an average of one every other day). We flew nearly a hundred combat hours during this month. This was not uncommon for that period; some crews exceed it for a longer period. With a few scrubbed missions thrown in, it seemed an endless succession of briefings and missions and interrogations. It was a pace that made old crews of new crews in a short time, considered from several angles. In some ways, it was good.

There is a second wind of nervous energy that can carry and sustain men beyond a normal expenditure and most crews found it during that month. Missions passed in an easy, endless blur and time was of no consequence. It was a continual round of falling into bed late in the afternoon and being routed out in the middle of the night. Only a rebellious, burning, crawling sensation in the pit of the stomach told you that you were tired.

For my crew, the longest stretch without at least a one-day break was a four-day succession of missions on the eighteenth, nineteenth, twentieth, and the twenty-first of June, to Hamburg, Bordeaux, Hamburg, and Berlin, respectively, for a total of thirty-six hours in the air. We were no more groggy than all the other operational crews of the group and on that fourth morning, but I remember the almost complete indifference I felt when I knew that Berlin was the target. That would certainly indicate that I was not in an entirely normal state at the time! Flying formation had become second nature to pilots. When you found yourself in the cockpit again you could hardly believe that it had been a whole day since you had performed those completely automatic actions.

Flight surgeons came around to barracks after missions and passed out sleeping pills to men who wanted them during those days of June. Men who felt they actually were not fit to fly on the next day, and they were very few, went to the station hospital, where they were allowed to sleep for a day before resuming the grind. I was fortunate in my sleeping habits and only took one pill for experiment, for I could always sleep where there was time for it.

No doubt each man had his own reactions to this test. For myself, the chief indication I had that I was living on an abnormal plane of nervous tension was the complete and burning impatience I often felt at small inconsequential things. And though I slept well I felt a gnawing restlessness the moment I had dressed on those rare days when we were on the ground. It might seem surprising to one who did not have this experience to know that a pilot or copilot could fall asleep during the fifteen or twenty minutes when the other pilot was flying. I could not have visualized it at the beginning of our missions but it came to that during June.

Possibly the biggest change in the actual nature of our operations came through the employment of the heavies for close-support bombing in the immediate front of the ground forces. This was done only on occasions of general or mass ground offensives, the most notable of which were on 18 July 1944, in cooperation with the British and Canadian attack in the Caen area, when 1,993 bombers and fighter-bombers of the Eighth and Ninth Air Forces dropped seven thousand tons of fragmentation bombs; and on 25 July 1944, in the great Operation Cobra, the breakthrough offensive of the First U.S. Army which preceded the historical dash of General Patton's Third Army through France.

In this latter operation, ground troops withdrew 1,200 yards to the north of the Periers-St. Lo Road and, beginning at 0940, three thousand heavy and medium bombers and fighter-bombers of the Eighth and Ninth attacked and saturated an area of few square miles with fragmentation bombs.

These close support missions were rather novel experiences for the crews of the heavies. They were flown at what were to them comparatively low altitudes—from twelve thousand feet, the lowest, to eighteen thousand feet. We felt that B-17s must have looked rather big to flak gunners at those heights. The greatest departure, however, from the long-range missions over Germany was the mental hazard of bombing so close to our troops. Prior to these missions, bombing had always been a coldly mathematical and scientific process, completely objective in nature. From the psychological viewpoint, it was strictly an impersonal operation. But the close support missions introduced the human element in a definite way, for inaccuracy or faulty judgment on the part of lead bombardiers and navigators not only would miss the target, but would result in death for some of the friendly ground troops.

Human error was not the only factor that could cause disaster, as was seen in Operation Cobra. There, a quirk or whim of nature in the form of a wind shift combined, perhaps, with an unsound judgment on the part of some bombardiers caused the deaths of a number of our ground troops. While wave after wave of heavies were crossing the front lines (marked chiefly by the broad Periers-St. Lo Road and red artillery bursts) and releasing their bombs in the target area, the wind shifted, carrying the pall of smoke from the bombed area back over the friendly troops. Some of the succeeding waves of bombers could identify the target area only by the smoke, and some combat boxes dropped on the smoke, which in certain sections was over our troops. Other lead bombardiers held their bombs and took them home. Instructions had been that unless the target area could be identified by the bombardiers, in accordance with all prearranged identification features, bombs would not be dropped.

Thus, in all these missions, the lead bombardiers were given a heavy responsibility. In the last few seconds of the bomb run, it was for them to decide whether their aim was positive and true and unmistakably on the aiming point, or whether it was too doubtful for them to release some fifty tons of explosives from their formation so close to friendly troops. They had to decide in a matter of a few seconds whether to waste the entire effort of the formation and take the bombs home, or to risk casualties to their own troops. It is no wonder that in hairline cases or in freakish situations such as this wind shift, the wrong decisions were sometimes made.

*   *   *

The mission on 25 July (Operation Cobra) I remember rather vividly for several reasons, but chiefly, perhaps, because it was on this mission that my crew came closest to being knocked down by a direct burst of flak. We flew as deputy lead of a combat box of twelve ships and went over the target at an altitude of fourteen thousand feet.

The flak was the climax of some other happenings which made it seem almost that we were not destined to go on that mission. They should be of interest in that they illustrate how crews sometimes managed to combat the boredom of routine long flight.

Shortly after our formation left the rendezvous point over England and headed for the coast, bombardier started the chain of events when he shorted an electrical circuit with the junction box cover of the chin turret assemblage while checking his equipment. He laid the cover aside, and he or "Mac"—in backing and turning in the confined space of the nose compartment—accidentally brought it in contact with some wires in such ways as to cause a short in the circuit. The result was a smoke-filled nose compartment and the start of a promising electrical fire. VE's voice had lost some of its accustomed nonchalance when he announced "fire in the nose!" over the interphone.

The interruption came at an unseasonable time. Jack was flying and I had just settled back in my seat and closed my eyes briefly, partly to impress him with my complete confidence in him and partly to indulge in one of those lofty reveries earlier mentioned. Nevertheless, VE's strident tones galvanized me. My left hand flipped off the battery and generator switches, and without saying good-bye to Jack (the fact that I left my parachute was possibly some assurance to him), I dropped down to the catwalk to see why VE was awake during his accustomed snooze period. Quick as I was, I trailed Ockerman who had skinned down from his turret at the first word and grabbed a fire extinguisher. Crouching in the catwalk, I saw that the fire was out in spite of the smoke and stench that filled the nose and was seeping back through the ship. Bombardier and Navigator were wiping smoke tears from their eyes, and VE pointed to some blackened wires in the chin turret junction box (the turret would be inoperative, but this was no reason for aborting this type of mission). Ockerman, with a relieved grin on his face, squeezed by me on his way to replace the fire extinguisher. For VE's benefit, he mouthed something about "firebugs"—remembering, no doubt, a similar fire in the nose of a ship at Dalhart, Texas.

I had scrambled around the narrow catwalk and started back to my seat when Ockerman fell into my lap and blurted "Number 3 and 4 are quittin'!" At the same time I felt the ship heel over to the right, away from the formation. I clawed by Ockerman and into my seat, somewhat taken aback by these multiplying events. Jack was in the middle of what appeared to be a very embarrassing situation—two engines out on one side with a full bomb load. He had pulled out of the formation and dropped below and, as I slid into my seat, was reaching for the feathering buttons. Automatically I reached down and flipped the battery and generator switches to the ON position. When I wheeled around, Jack was staring at the instrument panel, and on his face was a rare blend of relief, exasperation, incredulity, and disgust. He knew what had happened and instantly I knew too.

When battery and generator switches came on, the engine instruments—tachometer, manifold pressure, etc.—registered normally, whereas they had not registered with the switches in the OFF position, because these instruments operated electrically. Jack had not see me cut the switches (emergency procedure for electrical fires) but he saw me cut them on again and he knew he had been duped.

As he afterward explained it in the face of some kidding, he had glanced at the instrument panel at the same time that the ship seemed to pull against him to the right. This curious coincidence had been his undoing, for his eyes very naturally fell on numbers three and four instruments. To his sweating consternation, the indicator hands had sunk far below the green (normal readings)—engines were out cold! Ockerman, looking over his shoulder, had seen the same thing and that was when he landed in my lap. The switches were on again before Jack had time to recover from his first shock; otherwise he would have found out what the trouble was after a few moments of extreme discomfort, for the ship still flew normally. This, however, is hard to be sure of in the first few seconds after peeling away a formation, for a pilot usually feels about like he has jumped off a cliff. He has very little feel of the airplane. This fact had helped to fool Jack about the engines and had given us the second scare of the day. He never quite forgave himself for this little faux pas but, under the circumstances, it was nothing, even for a pilot who knew the engineering features of the plane as well as he did.

By this time, of course, those in the rear of the ship had begun to show some interest in the strange proceeding up front. A stench of something burning had seeped to the rear and that combined with our sudden departure from the formation had raised a healthy curiosity. Ball turret inquired bluntly over interphone as to what was happening and I told him everything was all right now. Perhaps my tone was not as reassuring as he desired, considering the happenings of the past few seconds. Miller, at any rate, had started through the bomb bay on a personal inspection when Ockerman waved him back. His eyes glistened from the dark recess of the bomb bay and I noted that his chute was bobbing on his chest as he turned around.

We pulled back into formation. But the day has started badly, and I was in no condition to hear what came over VHF. There had been some babbling on VHF due to the questionable weather conditions and the broken cloud deck which was at bombing altitude. There had been considerable talk, necessary transmissions, about changes in the bombing altitude. During assembly, it had been changed from "briefed plus one" (the briefed altitude plus one thousand feet) to "briefed" again. In an amazing and rare breach of radio discipline, a garrulous voice inquired as to whether bombing was to be at fourteen thousand feet. The answer would have been yes had he been answered, and this simple query sent chills down many a spine.

I flipped on interphone in time to hear Mac's reaction. "Start another fire, Brown," he growled. "Let's go home." At that time, a fire—or at least one dead engine—seemed preferable to going over target at an announced altitude of fourteen thousand feet.

That was probably the longest bomb run we were ever on, even if we didn't drop the bombs. I once heard a friend, who admittedly was a little flak-happy at the time, say that he could see the flash of the AA guns on the ground. And I thought that he had wronged even his keyed-up imagination in making this statement, but as we drove down this valley, I—for the first time—saw flashes on the ground and had that feeling, multiplied a hundredfold, of expecting a blow on the head or back. With each twinkle of light on the ground—which for all I know now, may have come from GI mess kits in the sun—I could visualize AA projectiles hurtling upward. And yet, for what seemed like hours, our formation plowed along on the bombing heading, bomb bay doors open and bombs hanging like overripe grapes in a breeze, and not a burst was fired at us. To our right and left, other boxes were receiving flak.

Navigator intoned the time: "Forty seconds—thirty seconds to go."

There was a muffled thud, and the ship surged upward. Three things registered almost simultaneously on me; two black splashes appeared in front of the lead ship, and I knew what the thud had come from. Ball turret called, "Number three pouring oil!" and Jack punched the feathering button on that engine and increased the prop pitch. My right hand gave an instinctive shove on the throttles, and we stayed in our place, with the number three prop feathered. For the time being, it was not necessary to jettison the bombs, and we could not have done so anyway, for we were over friendly troops until the bomb release point was reached.

For a few long seconds more we hung there, waiting for the bombs to go. Then, slowly, the doors on the lead ship closed, and we started a turn to the right. Our lead bombardier had decided not to drop, and we were going home with the bombs. In the last seconds before the turn, a burst had almost obscured the right wing of the lead ship, and shortly afterward, its number three prop whirled to a stop. It may have looked like a case of sympathy, but indeed it was not.

In fifteen minutes or less, we were over the channel and headed home. Engineer discovered a hydraulic leak, and we jettisoned the bombs as an extra precaution for a no-brake landing. Jack and I looked at a shattered and splintered place the size of a baseball on the windshield in front of him, and we thanked Providence that Sergeant Hirsch had found and installed a bulletproof window a few days before. We had been lucky again, for had we been three hundred miles inside Germany with that one engine shot out, things might have been more difficult. And thanks to Hirsch's newly installed windshield, Jack and I would never know which of us that piece of flak would have been coming for.

When we landed and examined the plane, we knew that the first burst, which had knocked out the engine, shattered the window, and disabled the hydraulic system, had indeed been close. Many holes of varying sizes on the underside and leading edge of the right wing showed that it had been below and slightly in front of the plane. As Croce put it, for a ranging shot it had not been a bad one.

Considering the events of the day, I had some doubt as to whether "milk run" was the proper term for these missions over Northern France. Further, there had been a growing suspicion among bomber crews that Northern France generally was a postgraduate school for flak gunners, and our poor, oil-splattered ship—victim of the very first salvo that had been fired at our formation—seemed to give supporting evidence to this suspicion.

*   *   *

Our contacts with the ground fighting on the continent were enhanced by frequent visits to our base by officers and men freshly returned from combat there. Late in June, some of the first paratroopers returned to England and filtered out to combat bases on visits to friends or relatives. It was amazing to see these men, just returned from the most brutal and bloody kind of ground battle, display childish enthusiasm and interest in our particular kind of combat.

Harry Baker's brother, who landed with the first paratroopers on D-Day, visited our base. He was bulging with tales of battle, with enemy souvenirs, and with an enormous enthusiasm to go on a combat mission. This worthy ambition could not be granted him, so he contented himself with inspecting our plane from nose to tail and with going out to the hardstand on two successive mornings to see us off on missions.

In those crowded days, poignant human drama unfolded. Another young paratrooper, fresh from battle on the continent, came to our base to visit his brother, whom he had not seen for two years. His brother, a tail gunner, was a veteran with only a few missions left in his tour. The visitor arrived at our base early one morning, but half an hour too late to see his brother, who had taken off on a mission.

All day, he waited. He was on the field when the formation returned. His brother's plane was pointed out to him as it landed and turned off the landing runway. He sensed that something was wrong when the ship came to a stop and an ambulance rushed out and drew up beside it. Then soon he knew: his brother was dead and frozen stiff in the tail of that plane, victim of the one piece of flak that had penetrated the plane over the target.

CHAPTER FIVE

LEAD CREW

5-1 Aircraft Commander—A view from the pilot's seat within the left side of the B-17 cockpit. The autopilot, located in the lower right corner of the photograph, was an important instrument for a successful bomb release. It could be linked to the Norden Bomb Sight, to enable the bombardier to "steer" the airplane through the sight on the last few seconds of the bomb run.

Source of photo: North Star Galleries

5-2 Bomb Sight—The top secret U.S. Norden Bomb Sight was the most accurate for its time. It was designed for high-altitude precision daytime bombing. The Norden Sight had precision optics linked to an analog computer and gyros that could connect with the autopilot in the B-17 cockpit. In the final moments of a bomb run, the pilot would turn control of the aircraft steering to the bombardier through the autopilot. Through the linkage of the bombsight to the autopilot, the bombardier would literally "fly" the bomber by manipulating the knobs on the bomb sight, until the bombs were dropped.

Source of photo: North Star Galleries

5-3 Autopilot—The C-1 Autopilot made it possible to achieve flight accuracy beyond human ability. It was invented by Honeywell Industries during WWII. The bombardier's linkage of the Norden Bomb Sight to the autopilot allowed for minute, accurate flight changes to be made on the bomb run to the enemy target.

Source of photo: North Star Galleries

5-4 Navigator—The navigator's station on the left side of the B-17 nose section is shown in the photograph, including the shelf for maps and charts and a .50-caliber machine gun nearby. The cramped nose compartment was shared by the bombardier and navigator. For lead crews to be successful, close coordination and anticipation among the two pilots, navigator, and bombardier was essential.

Source of photo: One Hundredth Bomb
Group Association website

First Lt. Robert A. Hand at the Gee-Box

5-5 Gee—The "Gee-Box" was an early type of electronic navigation, especially useful in cloud-covered missions. The navigator could set the coordinates of the destination into the Gee-Box. A series of cursers would intersect when the location was reached, in accordance with the coordinates set by the navigator. The photograph shows a navigator, First Lt. Robert A. Hand of the 303rd Bomb Group using a Gee-Box.

Source: 303rd Bomb Group Association "Hell's Angels"

5-6 Fortress Formation—A view of B-17 Flying Fortress in a group combat box formation with high and low elements, as illustrated earlier in chapter 2, figure 2-10. These Fortresses are from the 389th Bomb Group and are headed to Neumunster, Germany (13 April 1945), shortly before the war's end.

Source: United States Air Force photo.

V. LEAD CREW

A two thousand bomber mission over Germany was a major task force operation. It was an aerial invasion and for its success it required all the coordination and timing normally associated with such an operation. Yet, of the pilots and copilots, navigators, bombardiers, and gunners who were flying these daily armadas in 1944, by far the greater percentage had not even begun their period of training when the Eighth Air Force began its token operations in 1942. Most of the men aboard had never been in a military aircraft when the war began. The pilots in any of these daily formations who had over one thousand hours in the air could certainly have been counted on your fingers and toes. This whole gigantic machine—the trained men and the bombers they flew—was a wartime product. It involved twenty thousand crewmen for the bomber force and approximately one thousand fighter pilots for the escort. The main difference between these missions and a small-scale invasion, such as that at Dieppe*, was the frequency and regularity of the bombing missions. The pattern had been worked out, the system established, the chain of command and responsibility clearly delineated. Thus, a major military offensive was carried out day by day, with such regularity and precision that few of us were moved to wonder just how it came about.

*   *   *

Selection, training and scheduling of lead crews was a paramount responsibility of group and squadron commanders. Each group selected and trained crews to lead the combat box or boxes which were put up by the group. Several of the best or more experienced crews were reserved for wing lead and flew only on those days when their group was scheduled to furnish the lead combat box of the airborne wing. The designation "Lead Crew" thus applied to crews which flew as combat lead box or deputy (high or low box of the airborne wing), or as wing lead if specifically designated. Certain

---

*   The Dieppe raid was an Allied attack on the German occupied portion of Dieppe on the north coast of France on 19 August 1942. Over 6,000 Canadian troops were supported by a few hundred British commandos, Royal Navy, and Air Force. The Allied forces had to retreat, suffering over 3,600 casualties. The Dieppe raid followed the disastrous English army invasion and evacuation from Dunkirk the previous year (1941).

other crews within each squadron were regularly assigned to squadron lead positions in the group box formation. Since for all lead positions the object was to use the best crews, squadron leads usually went to the more experienced, the "older" crews of the squadrons. In most of 1944, the turnover or rotation of crews was so fast, with the intensive scale of operations, that combat experience was at a premium. The pace of missions was such that in two months time most crews found themselves transformed from greenhorns to veterans. With this accelerated pace, a great number of crews had a chance to fly squadron lead, at least during their last missions.

Group commanders and flying officers on the group staff, squadron commanders, operations officers, and other such key personnel always flew in lead positions; the group commander always as a wing leader or air division leader and squadron commanders and others as either wing or box lead. These flyers did not have assigned planes or crews of their own and they usually flew in the copilot seat with the lead crew (the regular copilot flew as tail gunner, filled in for another crew, or stayed on the ground). These key officers were not allowed to fly their missions on the same scale as the combat crews. Two or three generations of crews would pass through a group and finish their missions in turn while the group commander and his staff slowly added to their total. It should be said in passing that this was no break for these officers. Assuming that a man would eventually fly a given number of missions anyway, it was much easier in many ways to fly those missions at a reasonably fast rate. Most officers in this situation would have preferred to fly missions regularly with a crew of their own, than to fly infrequently, and each time with a different crew.

When group and squadron commanders flew in lead positions, there was no departure from the normal thing to be expected. But there was a rather unique feature about these formations: a second lieutenant or a first lieutenant who was pilot of a box lead crew often flew with his regular copilot and without this command copilot and was, therefore, in absolute and unmistakable command of the twelve or eighteen ships of his formation, for it was a first essential of air discipline that no ship should leave a formation except by necessity. He led these ships, and their success or failure on the mission—as well as considerable responsibility for their chance of a safe return home—lay with him and his crew, even though in the group he occupied no office of command whatsoever. In this one respect at least, air force combat was radically different from any other.

The reason, of course, was that successful command of a combat box hinged most of all on flying skill and proficiency; these were the prerequisites and the guarantees of success. The skill required here was almost solely a technical skill. The leader of a high or low box in a wing formation did not normally make any tactical decisions in the air. He applied his flying skill toward obeying the wing leader and maintaining his box in the wing formation. Such decisions as he made were more on the reflexive order, the spontaneous, instinctive actions and reactions of a good pilot to situations in flight as they occurred. The success of his lead depended more on his technical skill (and his crews), and on his general flying ability, than it did on any mature knowledge or training for military leadership. The characteristics of a leader were there, but the military training not always. In short, a twenty two or three year old kid who was a good pilot, and otherwise a normally levelheaded young man, often made a very capable combat box lead, even though his military background for such a position of responsibility was strictly limited. He occupied a position of great responsibility in the air by reason of his flying ability, but on the ground he was literally as well as figuratively, one of the boys.

*   *   *

There were many very excellent pilots, bombardiers, and navigators who never flew in a lead position and this was because they happened not to be on a crew which was a combination of all these. A good pilot with a mediocre navigator or bombardier, or both, did not make a good lead; nor did an excellent bombardier with a mediocre pilot and navigator. Either of the three was badly handicapped if the other two, or one of the two, did not measure up to high standards in his performance, or if the three of them did not cooperate to the fullest. Of course, every man on a crew was important to every phase of its missions, in countless little ways, which often became apparent only through failure; but in thinking of lead flying, we can consider only these three, for it was between them primarily that the formation was led and the bombs were dropped. When we speak of pilot, we refer to the two pilots in the cockpit of a bomber, for they were both there because it was a two man job of flying.

A good crew, a capable and dependable lead crew was one in which these three men were well trained and proficient in their special tasks, and where they cooperated with each other to a high degree. And that was not as simple an order as it might sound.

But for the excellent, the above-average lead crew—for the crew which consistently led the formation smoothly and expertly and consistently dropped the bombs on the target—there was an additional element of a more intrinsic nature, which might be called spontaneous coordination of personalities. This was a quality that could not be built into a team of men. Some of the chance assortment of ten, which were assembled in the training command, had this blessed blending of personality to a high degree; others had it to a lesser extent. This was something over and above the comradeship and loyalty that existed in all crews. It was something that enabled a certain combination of men to more readily understand each other, and to anticipate each other in the crucial moments of a combat mission.

The three ingredients of a successful bombing mission were good formation flying, exact navigation, and accurate bombing. These elements were inextricably related, and the degree of excellence of one depended upon the manner of performance of the other two essentials. The jobs of the pilot, the navigator, and the bombardier were inseparably dependent upon one another.

Navigation of a combat wing could not be a matter of approximation. Routes were plotted to close limits between known flak areas, and the slightest deviation from the prescribed course in distance or direction could often bring heavy penalty to a formation. The calculations were in the navigator's hands, and the execution was in the hands of the pilot. It was divided responsibility, and there was no way that it could be otherwise. The two men, in order to achieve the nearest approach to perfection, must not only willingly cooperate to the fullest, but they must be able—through association and practice—to anticipate each other's difficulties and, sometimes, to compensate each other's errors.

When a formation droned along at prescribed altitude on course and moved into cloud or contrail conditions, the pilot was sometimes forced to change course irregularly in order to keep his formation in the clear. In extreme conditions, he sometimes had to change airspeed and altitude. All of his attention and all of his skill was required if he were to have consideration for the ships in his formation and make the changes as smoothly as possible so that the formation remained intact. At such time, his sole concern was for the formation, and he had no time for navigation.

The navigator—seeing that this was happening—watched the compass, noted the changes of course, checked his watch, and calculated the total effect of deviation from the course. When the weather condition was cleared and course resumed, the navigator knew what total change of position had been effected and could quietly and efficiently give the pilot instructions to achieve correction. This is only one example of the many situations which required instinctive cooperation.

For accurate bombing, this cooperation through understanding between navigator and the bombardier was absolutely essential. The popular conception of our bomb sight was that with this instrument one man could drop bombs from great heights and hit his target consistently, provided he turned the knobs correctly. True, this turning of the knobs on the part of the bombardier was the culmination and the crux of the whole act of bombing; but it was by no means the whole operation, or any more important than some other operations which preceded it. The turning of the knobs, the final adjustments of the crosshairs in the sight, the last minute corrections of course and rate, were certainly crucial last acts, and unless the bombardier did them skillfully, all the important steps which had preceded this would come to nothing. But on the other hand, all the skill in the world could not make these last corrections on the bomb sight pay off unless bombardier and navigator and pilot had worked together as a team.

The pilot's job in this bombing operation was to fly the ship at the exact bombing altitude, at the exact airspeed which had been prescribed for bombing; and, further to lead the combat box with such smoothness that the other ships could maintain their places in formation on the bomb run and drop their bombs on the lead ship's release. The degree to which he failed in this was reflected in direct proportion on the bombing results. If his altitude or airspeed was off to any appreciable extent the bombing would not be entirely accurate, even if the bombardier had been perfect in his sighting; and if he had made the movements of his plane abrupt or violent, the formation was not to be as closely packed as it should have been and the bombing pattern would be large and irregular, even though the strikes of his own bombardier were right on target. The pilots control over the formation was especially important in the last turn to the heading of the bomb run. If this turn were carefully judged and well executed the formation rolled out of the turn with every ship in its place and there was very little last minute jockeying on the bomb run. It can be easily seen that if any of the wing ships of the formation were in violent or irregular motion, such as was necessary to regain position at the last minute, the bombs of that ship would not fall in the proper place, even if the plane itself were approximately in position. The irregular motion of the ship at the time of release would literally sling the bombs wide of the target.

After the bombardier "took over" with the sight and the autopilot, the pilot and copilot made those constant small adjustments of power and of autopilot control knobs which were necessary to keep the airspeed and altitude constant. It was an intensive job and it required all the attention of both of them during the few minutes of a bomb run and they were on interphone, listening to the last minute conversation between bombardier and navigator; ready to take over and fly the ship manually, following the bombardier's corrections on the PDI*, in case the autopilot should fail in the last few seconds. (This was not common, but it could, and did, happen sometimes; when it did, the cooperation of a crew received a severe test.)

When the formation turned on the bomb run, the vital time of navigator-bombardier cooperation was at hand. The job of hitting a target was often easier for the bombardier than finding the target. Once he had it in the bombsight, a reasonably proficient bombardier was sure to put some bombs on the target, but the difficulty was in finding and identifying it in time to get a good sight picture and make the last minute corrections. This was where careful prior study of target pictures and pictures of surrounding terrain and features paid off; but most of all, this was where the navigator could give invaluable help. Sometimes the navigator could steer him onto the target by simple pilotage while he made last minute checks of his equipment. He could help right up to the last act of sighting and if he did help, the last act of sighting and quick correction was a much smoother and surer process. If the navigator assisted the bombardier in getting the formation lined up quickly on the approximate heading to the target, even when the target itself could not yet be seen, the bombardier was likely to be able to spot the target at the earliest possible moment, and, equally important, he would not have to make violent corrections at the last moment.

---

*   PDI—Pilot Directional Indicator on the instrument panel.

The final moment before bomb release was the climax of the mission—the reason and the end. It was the payoff for all the many painstaking plans, and the whole effort of the mission. The whole act of bombing was a cooperative thing, and it was hard to say where the responsibility rested primarily. Certainly, the final and ultimate act for success or failure was done by the bombardier. His last feather touch on the course knob before the automatic release of the bombs was the sharp point of a wedge which represented the combined efforts of all.

*   *   *

All we have said has been from the standpoint of successful leading—smooth formation flying and perfect bombing. We have said what was necessary to this desired precision and perfection and have, therefore, risked suggesting that perfection was always achieved. But this, of course, was not true; there was no such thing as the perfect mission, though there were many creditable approaches to perfection. There was always some phase of a mission that could have been better.

There were, of course, cases of complete and drastic failure on the part of formation leaders, and these failures sometimes resulted in needless loss of planes and crews. This was inevitable. But aside from these debacles, few in number, there were the more numerous cases and partial failure—or rather, incomplete success on the part of leaders. No lead crew could begin by being experienced and entirely proficient, and the skill which it developed was attained through actual combat experience.

Leading in any capacity—leader of a flight of three, a squadron of six, or combat box of twelve—had many flight problems for a pilot. Each of these lead positions was different and had its own difficulties. Normally, a pilot and a crew progresses gradually from one lead position to the other in the order named, but in each position of lead, no matter how much experience had been acquired in another capacity, new situations and new experiences were met. The manifold factors of relative speed, judgment of distance, angles and rate of turn, relative wind differential (in the case of combat box leading), and proper anticipation of the lag and surge of a heavily loaded ship within a formation were mastered gradually, and they were applied in a slightly different way in each of these lead positions.

The pilot and the navigator were the two men who were really on the spot in lead flying. While the bombardier's work was the crux of the whole mission, the fact that he hit the target or missed it did not affect the safety of the other planes in the flight. But if the navigator led the formation over a flak area and ships in the formation were lost or damaged, he felt very badly, and so did everyone else concerned. And if the pilot, through a lack of judgment or poor flying technique, made formation flying more difficult for the ships of his formation than it should have been, the pilots in his formation were inclined to take a very dark view of him after about eight or nine hours in the formation. Often, of course, much unjust and heated criticism and some very stinging profanity were hurled at a leader from the privacy of oxygen masks by the pilots in his formation, who were sometimes experiencing troubles over which the leader had no control. Fortunately for his peace of mind, these comments never reached his ears, and unless he had done a really bad job, a lead pilot was not likely to hear any criticism from his fellow pilots on the ground. We all knew that we were inclined to be unjustly critical after long hours in the air, and we knew that formation flying was bound to be hard work on a long mission, no matter who was leading.

Nevertheless, a pilot or navigator felt rather sheepish when he returned from a mission where things had not gone well, whether he was actually to blame or not. There probably was not one lead navigator or pilot who did not, at one time or another, feel red in the face and apologetic because he had not done as well as he should have or as he wanted to do.

One of the best and most conscientious navigators in our group walked around with a hang-dog air for weeks because he let our formation run into some surprise flak one day. He was leading a combat box, which was returning from a mission to Paris-Le Bourget Field. The return route was almost, if not exactly, the reverse of the route in. We had encountered no flak on the trip in to the target, and our formation was well on the way back to the coast. The lead navigator had deftly weaved our box in and out and around all suspected danger points on the way in and was doing the same on the way back out. He was probably rechecking his ETA for the coast and indulging in some inward satisfaction at the time that he and the formation had a very rude awakening.

Flak began thumping into the formation in an amazingly accurate barrage. It was so unexpected and so accurate that the planes momentarily scattered like a flock of geese fired on from the blind. The lead ship lost one engine and wallowed briefly in the barrage until the pilot got things under control and skidded out and away. The ships reassembled beyond the flak area and continued homeward, with nothing more serious than a couple of feathered engines and numerous flak holes in most of the ships. Considering the fine accuracy of the barrage, it was miraculous that none of the planes were shot down, and only the lead navigator and his crew will ever know how thankful they were that none of them were lost.

Of course, the lead navigator could hardly have been blamed for the debacle, no matter how many ships had been lost. He was on course on the prescribed route at the time, and in the briefing, there had been no flak indicated at the tiny village from which it apparently came. It was just another case of the Germans shifting some of their batteries—which they continuously did in Northern France—and catching a formation by surprise.

*   *   *

The most excruciating, nerve-wracking hours I spent in combat flying were on a mission to Bordeaux as leader of the low squadron of a combat box. This was one of the first squadron lead flights for my crew and, unfortunately for us, we never led a squadron under worse conditions. This was one of the days when weather was of that unpredictable nature that it seemed to build up around formations as they moved along. It was a day of heavy contrails, which literally built mists and clouds in and among the formations even after they had climbed above twenty thousand feet. It was virtually impossible for formations to remain closely packed as they moved through the worst of it over Northern France, and it developed that most of the boxes became separated, with the hope of reassembling when the contrails dissipated at bombing altitude.

Soon after we crossed the French coast and headed down over the heart of France, I found myself leading a lone squadron through a void of mists and fogs. For a new squadron lead, this was disconcerting, even though I could tell from the babble on the VHF that the same thing had happened to many other squadrons. The only thing to do—and the obvious thing—was to continue the climb on the prescribed course with the hope of breaking out into the clear within sight and reach of the other squadrons of my box. I had flipped on the pitot tube heater as we crossed the channel and began to encounter the heavy contrails. This was supposed to insure that the pitot static tube would remain clear of ice and that the airspeed indicator would register accurately. But soon, the airspeed indicator began a mad and erratic dance which indicated that the heater was not working adequately and that ice was alternately blocking and clearing the pitot tube.

This was instrument flying at its best, and at its worst. With an airspeed that could not be depended upon, instrument flying was twice as hard. Before I actually knew what was happening to the airspeed, I think that I practically stalled the ships of the formation by pulling up into too steep a climb. Then, realizing what I had done, I plumped them down again until, finally, we settled into something like an even, smooth climb. Copilot and I had to rely on the gyro artificial horizon, the very undependable rate-of-climb indicator, and power setting since the airspeed indicator was definitely not to be trusted.

During that endless vacuum of time when we were boring upward through the clouds and mist, I experienced an almost-overpowering urge, which I feel sure has been experienced by every pilot at one time or another in instrument flying: the urge to give up, to let off and plunge downward through the void until, somewhere below, I would break out in the clear. Normally it would not be considered a desirable situation to be above a cloud deck at twenty-five thousand feet with one lone squadron deep over enemy territory, yet we could have shouted with joy when we finally broke into the clear at that altitude.

Here was a case where a navigator had made up for the unavoidable difficulties of the pilot. With our many troubles, Jack and I had certainly not been able to fly an exact course; the best that could be said for us is that we weaved back and forth from one heading to another, with variations of ten degrees more or less, and that we approximated the correct heading on an average. "Mac" had checked us constantly, and by using his watch and judging the airspeed, from knowing what it normally would be in a climb, he had a surprisingly good idea as to where we were when we broke out, as it developed. He gave me a heading and we barreled along, still trailing our five original ships, surprisingly enough.

VHF was now alive with chatter of box leaders and squadron leaders trying to get together again. I heard Woodcraft White, our wing leader calling Woodcraft Red—who was Opie, my box leader for the day—and telling him to pull his formation up and join the lead box for the bomb run. By this time, I knew that high squadron had also been shaken off and had not yet found its place again. The chatter indicated that most of the wings had become separated and that they were now in the process of reforming. I was in a fever as we cruised along toward the turning point, for we had gotten behind and it would be a very close thing if we managed to intercept the formation at the turning point or even on the bomb run. The tiny dots ahead grew larger, and I gloated over the fact that we were on the inside track, so to speak; when they turned in on the bomb run, they would turn to the right, and we were somewhat off course to the right. We could intercept them.

When we had approached close enough to distinguish ships and parts of the formation—losing altitude all the time since we had climbed somewhat above bombing altitude to get out of the clouds—we saw that Opie was still dragging along behind and below the lead box, evidently in the hope that his two lost squadrons would catch up with him. And, as a matter of fact, we screeched into our place below Opie's formation just as the wing was turning on the bomb run. I say we "screeched" for we were going at something above normal prescribed speed in order to catch up, and I was too abrupt for a squadron lead when we slackened speed and joined the formation again as the low squadron. So abrupt was I that my left wing ship, which was on the outside of the turn onto the bomb run, was literally flung off into space. I saw it staggering and wallowing a hundred yards off our wing as the bomb bay doors began to come open. We settled down on the bomb run and, looking up, I saw to my amazement that the high squadron had also appeared from nowhere and settled into space. Our wing was intact as we headed for the target. The wing ship, which I had unceremoniously flung off, rejoined us and tucked himself into his place in time to get his tail shot off by a direct burst of flak. The ship was flown by Lieutenant Fillmier and his new crew, and this was their second or third mission. I happened to be glancing toward the ship at the time a burst shattered its tail and it plunged abruptly downward. I never expected to see these men again and, there on the bomb run, I momentarily regretted that through force of circumstances, we had given them such a rough ride on their last mission.

The rest of the mission, hellish though it was, was an anticlimax to what happened up to that point. Flak was intense on the bomb run, but Fillmier's ship was the only one shot down out of the box. We were forced to climb to thirty thousand feet on the way back to stay above the weather and keep the formation intact. After some seven hours, almost all of it on oxygen, most of it instrument flying, a lot of flak, it was maddening to sit up there at thirty thousand feet over this endless plain of clouds. All things considered, this was certainly one of the most exhausting missions of our entire tour.

When we found ourselves on the ground again, we were all too exhausted and too relieved to worry much about what had happened on the mission. And we knew, too, that formation flying in the conditions we had encountered that day was bound to be a nightmare experience, and there was no way around it. But I still felt somewhat like a schoolboy before the principal when I went to the barracks and found old LaFeavor, leader of my second element lying on his bunk, picture of utter exhaustion. When I had called LaFeavor on VHF and asked him what his airspeed read, he replied that it was "out." That, apparently, was because we had pulled up into such a steep climb temporarily (because my airspeed actually was out), that LaFeavor had at first disbelieved his indicator, which was registering something like 115 mph.

But LaFeavor, back safe and sound on his bunk, was feeling inclined to make light of his trials of the day. He looked at me wryly and said, "Boy, I wish I could slow-fly a B-17 like you can!"

CHAPTER SIX

INCIDENTAL THINGS

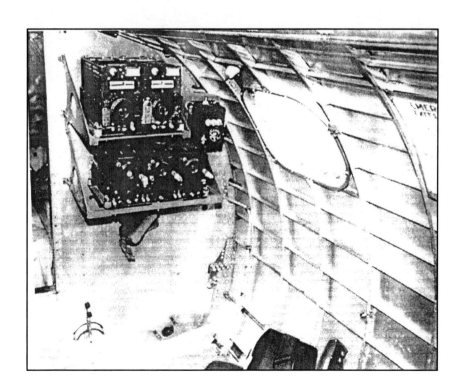

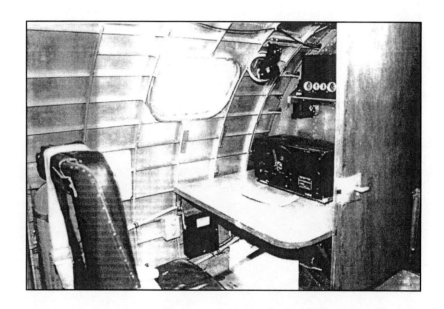

6-1 Radio Compartment—The communications and electronic defense system of the B-17 Flying Fortress was aft of the bomb bay. The left and right sides of the radio operator's station is shown in this figure, looking forward to the front of the aircraft and the bombs. Without intra-crew communications and external communication with other aircraft in the formation and home base, a mission would not be successful.

Source: 457th Bomb Group Association.org

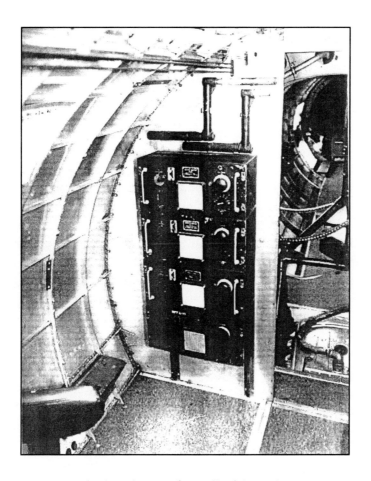

6-2 Jammers—Attached to the rear firewall of the radio compartment were three transmitters designed to "jam" (disrupt) enemy radar signals tracking the bomber formations. At the bottom was a receiver that detected the radar signal. Once the signal was picked up, the jamming transmitters could be used simultaneously against several radar sites. The B-17's radio system was a defensive system, as well as for communication. The radio operator could also use a single .50-caliber machine gun for enemy-fighter defense.

Source: 457th Bomb Group Association.org

VI. INCIDENTAL THINGS

Many things contributing to the total of impressions and recollections from a tour of bomber combat might at first seem incidental. The two words *fighter* and *flak* are a key to the popular conception of aerial combat. We who have flown even a few missions would be the last to deny the significance of these words, but know that they were only a part of the experience.

Truly had it not been for fighters and flak, many crews might have succumbed to the utter boredom and weariness of the last few hours of a ten hour mission. Ten hours of sitting cramped and cold in one place, ten hours of sucking oxygen from a tube, then hours of exacting formation flying; these things did not kill us, but they soon wore us down. Flak and fighters during the few minutes we dealt with them called forth the adrenalin which sustained us through the long hours. Many other factors were part of a combat mission. Some were aggravations; some furnished a little amusement, which helped to beguile the hours.

*   *   *

I found both frustration and amusement in the use of radio communications. This of course, was a way of life in flying operations. The radio headset, the jack box, and constant monitoring of internal or external communication were all together part of our lives. In assigning code names, the communications powers gutted the vocabulary of our language in their attempt to assign suitably mysterious or noncommittal designations to all stations for security purposes. One who by the nature of his work was forced to sit long hours on radio watch soon became callous to the many strange or incongruous phrases or combinations of code words which have been surprising, and, even to us who sometimes come to hate the sight of a pair of earphones, they were often amusing. These are some conversational fragments typical of what you might have heard in the course of a few hours in the air on radio watch.

"Hello, Ripsaw 2—this is Woodpile calling."

And if that is not startling, wait for the reply, which comes rasping back after a short interval. "Hello, Woodpile. This is Ripsaw 2, come on in."

A rather dubious invitation, this, if taken literally, but really not so bad. A fighter-bomber is calling the ground controller radio and has now been acknowledged and cleared for further transmission. In fact, in this case, the fighter will be the ripsaw (figuratively speaking), and the ground controller will vector or direct him to some choice enemy target for destruction.

"Hello, Wideworld—this is Prodigal calling," we hear; and Wideworld answered in the pleasing feminine voice of a British WAAF, which might well be contrived to lure the Prodigal into further conversational wanderings.

It so happens, though, that Worldwide in this case is the home field for the Prodigal son, and he is calling for landing instructions. Soon we hear him again, "Wideworld, this is Prodigal, on approach with wheels down. Am I clear for landing?"

And the blithe, airy response: "Prodigal, clear to pancake."

A nice thing to hear after a long tiresome flight, in any tone of voice.

One afternoon on a training flight over England, I sat and punched from channel to channel on VHF, listening to the variety of radio chatter. Then even my hardened ears were shocked, when I heard in a strangely sepulchral voice, "Hello, Bloodstream. Hello, Bloodstream. This is Brutus calling." And then again, in slow, monotonous insistence. "Hello, Bloodstream. Hello, Bloodstream. This is Brutus calling." The enunciation was slow and deliberate, and the tone was grave. Certainly, it was appropriate for a voice from the past, which had been echoing and reechoing through the centuries and now was caught at last. It should have been a ghost from dim history, but in all reality, it probably was some American kid new to England and the radio procedure who made it a fetish to be deliberate and exact.

Thinking of code names, our recent experience comes to mind. When we departed Greenier Field, New Hampshire, in the new B-17 which we ferried over the Atlantic, our ship was given the rather dashing code name of Harem Mike. The other twenty odd ships making this consignment flight all had their individual code names, which were to be the official identification for the ships during the crossing. There was Item How, Able Charlie, Oboe Peter, Queen Roger, and other such phonetic combinations.

And during the first leg of the flight to Gander Lake, Newfoundland, we could identify some of these noncommittal names by the familiar voices which sounded them in the routine check-in calls to ground stations. I thought Harem Mike was a more imaginative and pleasing code name than most of the others and was well pleased with. It had a nice sound, and it seemed to give this ship—which was otherwise AC# 437272—a little personality.

Harem Mike put in a somewhat dramatic appearance at Gander Lake, Newfoundland, late on the afternoon of 26 March. We had been the last ship to take off from Greenier Field, having been delayed by mechanical trouble, and when we were arrived over Gander Lake, all the other ships had landed and a solid blanket of clouds was building up to ten thousand feet. As is often the case under bad weather conditions, radio was poor and we lost contact with the tower after being cleared for an instrument letdown. We did not receive him again until we broke out of the clouds at three hundred feet in very poor visibility.

The field was in sight just ahead, and we were congratulating ourselves and wiping the sweat from our brows when a flurry of snow blotted our visual contact completely. In a matter of seconds, we completely lost the field in the monotonous landscape and the fluctuating visibility. I still remember the rising note of anxiety—the almost frantic tone that welled up in the tower operator's voice as he called again and again, seeking to gain contact and learn our whereabouts. For some reason known only to the radio transmitter, our voice transmission had failed at this critical time. And so he wailed on: "Harem Mike, Harem Mike, what is your position? What is your position?" And in the meantime, Harem Mike scuttled around between the ceiling and the spruce trees like a mad fox in a henhouse. A B-17 can be maneuvered in close places, but this was confining. We made a wide, swooping circuit over the trackless waste of snow and spruce, came over the range station again, and flew the compass heading back to the field. Even then, Harem Mike made two thundering, window-shaking passes at the field in the gathering murk and darkness and, no doubt, rattled the teeth of the tower operator on the second one. The second time around, Harem Mike found the runway and lurched in for a landing as the snow flurries came faster and heavier. Something closely akin to a sigh of relief preceded the tower's taxiing instructions, given as he saw that we were definitely on the runway. He was worried!

On combat missions, VHF (radio) sometimes drove a man to distraction and at other times gave him a lifesaving laugh. There was humor and grim drama on VHF! Any radio program with a flair for the sensational would have had something if it could have cut in on a bomber channel during the progress of a mission. Voices had a disembodied characteristic, which divorced them from time or place.

After eight hours in the air, I have heard voices which made me grind my teeth and commit murder in my heart; slurring, incomprehensible voices; quarrelous voices; plaintive, squealing voices; rasping voices. On the other hand, I have heard cool, confident voices, which were a steady hand in the darkness—the call of Air-Sea Rescue answering a bomber's plea, or the response of the home tower. Invariably these voices from the ground carried a suggestion of security and relaxation. The tone and inflection brought a picture to the mind. The listener formed a mental impression of the speaker and instinctively liked or disliked him.

Sometimes VHF conversations sounded strangely out of place, particularly some of those which took place during assembly on mornings of bad weather. In listening to them, one might have felt that a wing leader was the "old lady who lived in a shoe and had so many children she didn't know what to do"—rather than the leader of a combat force in process of assembly.

I recall an exchange that went about like this:

"Woodcraft Charley, this is one of your children. Will you fire a flare?" in a piping voice.

"This is Woodcraft Charley—firing a flare!" in a strong, somewhat impatient tone.

Silence for a few moments, and we know that somewhere in the contrails and heavy clouds, a plane is groping for sight of its leader.

Again, our Piping friend: "Woodcraft Charley, this is one of your children. Will you fire another flare?"

"Woodcraft Charley—firing a flare." He sounds a little more impatient this time. Woodcraft Charley has troubles of his own in keeping his wing of planes together under these weather conditions, and he had no time for stray children who are lost. It is almost time to leave the rendezvous point anyway.

"Woodcraft Charley, this is one of your children. Will you please fire another flare?"

"This is Woodcraft Charley. If you haven't found me by now, go back home," replies an exasperated voice from space.

"Roger," says the meek little voice.

VHF discipline required that only necessary transmissions be made. The enemy was always listening, and any unguarded transmissions could have been useful to him. Yet when unusual conditions prevailed, particularly adverse weather, the bomber-to-bomber channel was often cluttered with voices from everywhere. Some transmissions could definitely be classed as unnecessary. Once, our wing was returning over Northern France from a mission. Normally the formation would have been down to a comfortable altitude where oxygen could be used in snatches, if at all. But because of heavy cloud conditions, the wing leader had elected to stay at twenty thousand feet. Some of the tail-end Charleys evidently disagreed with his decision. Nerves and tempers were frayed after six hours on oxygen.

"Woodcraft White Leader, I'm short on oxygen. When are we going down?" demanded a plane of the formation.

"Oh, don't you know? We like it up here," rasped an unidentified voice reeking with sarcasm, evidently from the rear of the formation.

*   *   *

Human nature doesn't change under stress. It simply becomes intensified. Between the moments of greatness are the long stretches when human nature operates as it always has (bless us all). We are thinking of the "spare" ships sent up by each group. These ships—two or three per group, usually—took off behind the formation and trailed it to the English coast. They were loaded with bombs and were in every way ready for the missions, but they were extra ships, over and above the formation requirements. If one or more of the ships in the formation aborted for any reason and turned home, the "spares" filled their places in the designated order. If not, the "spares" turned around at the coast and came home—and had no mission for all their trouble. This was a chore divided fairly among all the crews.

These crews attended briefing, of course, and therefore knew what kind of mission was in store for the day. If the mission was a long, tough grind, the "spares" privately hoped that all their trouble and work would go for naught, and they would have to turn around at the coast. At the same time, they knew that their chances of going on that mission were excellent, for a pilot and crew would turn around more quickly for mechanical reasons from a tough one, which would keep them over enemy territory a long time, than they would a relatively short mission, where the hazard was not so great. If the mission was a short one over Northern France, the "spares" gnashed their teeth, for they knew how small their chances were of getting on the mission. It was a vicious circle for the "spares," and they stood to lose in any case.

The behavior of these planes in the air usually illustrated the situation. If the mission was going to Munich, for example, they skulked along behind on the route out to the coast, each one of the two or three jockeying for the rearmost or most inaccessible spot, each willing to concede another the first opening in the formation. They were suggestive of Shakespeare's "Whining schoolboy, with his satchel and shining morning face, creeping like a snail unwilling to school." And the instant the formation crossed the coast and the letter of the law was complied with, such spares as were left turned tail and went home.

But if the mission was a "milk run"—a short one with little opposition expected—things were different. All the way to the coast, spares hung over the formation, swooping and turning, searching for any opening. They wheeled like vultures over any prospective aborting planes and dogged the formation to within sight of the enemy coast. Any latecomer or straggler was apt to find his place taken by an eager "spare."

*   *   *

Gunners were hard judges of formation flying. These men sat back in their turrets and sweated when their plane struggles in formation. They knew what happened to stragglers, and they liked to see the formation close around them. They liked to see their pilot tuck his plane in close and fly a good formation. They took pride in it, and it added to their peace of mind. A pilot who borrowed or was assigned a gunner from another crew for a mission had a very severe, though unspoken, critic aboard his plane that day. The guest gunner would be predisposed to find the strange pilot lacking in the finer points of flying as evidenced at all times by his own pilot. That was a fine thing. They believed in their pilots and championed them loyally on all occasions.

But few of them were above dropping a gentle hint if things were not going to please them, even if the hint went to the ears of their own pilot. One morning, on one of our earlier missions, when Jack and I were not in on all the tricks of formation flying, we experienced difficulty in maintaining our position in the second element of the low squadron—a hard position and an undesirable one at best. Our superchargers were not producing full power, and we were falling behind. We were over enemy territory and in the last stage of our long climb to bombing altitude. We were ripe for fighter attack. The fidgety silence on interphone was broken.

"Top turret to tail gunner."
"Go ahead."
"Kinda lonesome back there, eh?"
"Yeah, sure is," in a shaky voice.

I could picture Baker crouched over his guns in the tail. At that point, he could have spotted a horsefly at a thousand yards. Relief needed no expression when the climb ended, and we regained our place in the formation.

The gunners were not only interested in the formation flying; they were often a great help to their pilots, particularly if the crew were flying as lead ship. The pilot of a squadron or box lead plane could not possibly see all the ships of his formation. Gunners who have been trained to it could give him invaluable assistance. Tail gunner could keep him posted on ships in the rear of the formation, and ball turret on those below. In short, a pilot who had learned to depend on his gunners to some extent and who had explained to them some of the problems and conditions of formation flying had acquired for himself a great deal of assistance and even more peace of mind.

When thirty-ton airplanes are flown in tight formation, stacked in layers fifty to one hundred feet apart, wing collisions were not an inconsiderable danger, no matter how good the pilots. Few, if any, combat pilots can look back on their missions without remembering a few conditions when they were saved from collision by an alert gunner who called danger in time.

When clouds and contrails closed in on a wing of bombers, the pilots had one of the most grueling jobs in the world. Then they must maintain their places in formation in a confusing void without top or bottom, dimensions, or shape. Vertigo stalked them. Wave after wave of blinding contrails swept over them and blotted out their vision. One instant the formation was turning away; the next instant, turning in; now it appeared to be climbing, now diving. It required the utmost in willpower and self-discipline to resist the almost overwhelming urge to correct violently for an assumed false altitude of the plane; to check flight instruments and believe them despite the evidence of all the senses. In such flying, pilots dripped sweat in cockpits that registered zero. This was the flying which required unspoken and unconscious cooperation between the two pilots of the plane. One flew, alternately on instruments and contact, eyes sweeping from instrument panel to the formation, with no thought or time for anything else; the other watched and checked everything in the cockpit, constantly made adjustments needed, but unasked; took over the controls at a word or a gesture.

On these bad days, we depended heavily on our gunners to see for us. While our attention was required fully in the task of flying and maintaining our place, the gunners warned us of danger from below, above, and behind. In our own case, Bob Ockerman, top turret gunner, once saved us from having our tail chewed off by a plane above and behind us.

Another time, however, this one hundred percent cooperation created a momentary confusion in the cockpit. Our formation was scudding north over the Bay of Biscayne at one thousand feet, returning from a mission to Southern France. The ceiling lowered unexpectedly, and visibility became very poor. The formation of thirty-six planes spread out and dropped lower—was soon flying at an altitude of two hundred feet in very poor visibility. No doubt, it was a thrilling spectacle to anyone who saw us from a boat, but to us aboard the planes, it was very uncomfortable and a hazardous experience. Prop wash was a serious thing at this low altitude, and adjacent planes appeared and faded uncertainly in the mist and rain. Bombardier sat in his plexiglas nose and watched the spray and waves just below him, warned us now and then to pull up a bit.

I was flying when, out of the corner of my eyes, I saw the plane on my left edging in toward us through the mist. Quickly, I skidded out to the right. At that instant, Miller yelled from the right waist, and copilot heaved against me on the controls. The plane on our right was also closing in. We couldn't go right or left, and certainly not down, so we were forced to climb. We continued the original heading and until we broke out on top of the cloud deck. This was the only time that Jack and I ever battled over the controls, and the result was a compromise in this case. A number of planes had already been forced to climb as soon the wing reformed on top.

*   *   *

Often, men's reactions in dire moments were surprising—even ludicrous. A plane of our group fought its way home "on the deck" from a deep penetration one day with one prop running away and another pulling only half power. It had been forced to leave formation and had lost altitude. The ship was shot at and hit by every caliber weapon the Germans could point in the air as she barged wildly along, headed in the general direction of home, plunging over airfields and other installations in her path. The gunners were frozen to their fifty calibers, spewing slugs at everything that looked hostile while pilot and copilot fought the plane along. Tail gunner sitting on his parachute, firing away, felt hot breath on his rear. Looking down he saw that the chute pack had been ripped open beneath him; a large hunk of something lethal had torn away part of the chute and part of his electrically heated flying suit. "My god, I'm hit!" he cried and rushed up to the waist of the ship. There, gesturing wildly and shouting above the roar and the din, he tried to make known his plight to the waist gunners. His right hand stroked where the seat of his pants had been and came away.

His eyes widened as they fell on a hand which should have been crimson. "Hell! No blood!" he yelled and scrambled back to the tail.

Strange and untimely images sometimes flashed on the mind in crowded moments. Once, I saw the azaleas of Magnolia Gardens, Charleston, South Carolina, from a height of five miles above the city of Munich, Germany. We were on the bomb run, and flak was blooming on invisible stems above the overcast. A break appeared, and I caught a glimpse of vivid splashes of red on the earth below, interspersed in the regular pattern of what appeared to be a giant park. Perhaps it was a park; perhaps it was a figment of my imagination. Strange that my mind should have flashed to springtime at home and azaleas blooming.

In one instant, the thought and the vision were gone—crowded out, we might say, by the affairs of the moment—for daydreaming on a bomb run is not standard practice. Later, I could not help but think that, as a last earthly image, this would not have been a bad one.

CHAPTER SEVEN

ONE DAY'S WORK

7-1 Riders on the Storm—A Flying Fortress group formation flies through a high-altitude field of deadly enemy antiaircraft artillery explosions, known as "flak."

Source: U.S. Air Force photo

7-2 Fliegerabwehrkanone (Flak)—A German 88-mm antiaircraft cannon and crew, pointing their weapon to the sky. Radar would detect the movement and altitude of the bomber formations, which was also relayed by aircraft following the bombers. Crews could then set the timing of fuses on their cannon shells to explode at the formation altitude, sending concussions and exploded metal into the planes. The 88-mm cannons were the most accurate and feared flak guns. The picture shows two other flak cannons in the background.

Source photo: Bundesarchive, 1943 photo

7-3 Briefing—Eighth Air Force bomber crews at a mission briefing in England (1944). A drawing of the German "Komet" jet rocket fighter is pinned on the large briefing map for identification.

Source: U.S. Air Force photo)

7-4 Big Bad Wulf—The German Focke-Wulf FW-190 fighter airplane. It was the fastest and most formidable of all enemy fighters attacking U.S. bomber formations. It was also used extensively for ground support in Russia and North Africa. A later version replaced the BMW radial engine with an in-line piston engine that was more powerful, enabling the plane to carry more weapons. The new engine required a longer fuselage, hence the Allied bomber crews nicknamed it "Long Nose."

Source: World War II Planes

7-5 Destroyer—The Messerschmitt Bf-110 Zorestorer (Destroyer) was a formidable twin-engine fighter-bomber. It was used for support of ground troops as well as attacking Allied bomber formations—the aircraft had 30-mm cannons and rockets to destroy bombers. It was even used to fly over the bomber formations and drop bombs on them. There was also a night-fighter version to attack the British Royal Air Force bombers on their night missions.

Source: Bundesarchive

7-6 The ME-109—The Messerschmitt Bf-109 (or ME-109) was the most common fighter of the Luftwaffe during WWII. It was developed in 1935 and first used in combat during the Spanish Civil War in 1937, and later in the Battle of Britain. It carried an array of machine guns and cannons to attack Allied aircraft.

Source: World War II Planes

7-7 Stragglers—Battle damaged bombers such as the ship in the top figure had a long, lonesome, and dangerous journey to home base. Often with dead or wounded airmen aboard. Those who reached home often had a hard landing, such as the B-17 in the lower figure, from the 401st Bomb Group.

Source: 401st Bomb Group website

7-8 Battle damage—As the B-17 and B-24 bombers were often horribly damaged, so were the humans inside. The G.I. flak protection helmet was pierced by metal from a Flak explosion. Dr. Hiram "Pop" Hardesty a 401st Group flight surgeon, helps a wounded airman from a B-17.

Source: 401st Bomb Group Association

VII. ONE DAY'S WORK

The lights come on and tear us from sleep. I look at my watch. It's 0230.

The orderly's voice sings the old refrain, "Breakfast at 0300, briefing at 0400, trucks in the area in fifteen minutes. Crews flying: Lieutenant Risher, Lieutenant LaFeavor, Lieutenant Grumman, Lieutenant Wilbur."

He takes a quick look around to see that we are awake and disappears. His is a dangerous job!

I look to the far corner of the barracks and see the blankets heaving on the bunks. The fellows are awake. I've slept soundly as usual, but it was instantly over here. The "sack" is good at 0230, but already I feel charged with energy and filled with a tense expectancy. As I dress, I hear movement and muttering in the far end of the barracks. I put on heavy socks and GI shoes, winter undershirt, shorts, woolen shirt, dark slacks, and necktie. I check my "dog tags" and feel for the escape photos* in my left shirt pocket. I take my "mission cap" from its nail and am ready to go.

"See you at the mess hall," I call to Jack, who is dressing on the edge of his bunk. "I'll pick up the truck."

At the orderly room, I draw a truck with Fred Taylor, "Uncle Fred." We walk out in pitch dark and climb in. The crews, except for the few dim figures clambering in with us, will walk to the mess; so we wave the driver on. The air is cool and damp and rich with country smells. There is an overcast. In the background—above the whine of the GI truck—is a muted, undulating roar. The crew chiefs are running up the engines on the line.

None of us are really awake until we hit the mess hall and have a slug of strong, hot coffee. We fall in line for our trays, pass along and pick up fried eggs, bacon, cereal, toast and jam. The mess hall is crowded, so it must be an ME (maximum effort) today. Jack, "VE," and "Mac" appear in a knot

---

*   Packet of pictures taken in civilian clothes, to be used for passport or visas, etc., in effecting escape if shot down. Furnished to all flyers.

of latecomers. Their faces bear the look of animation and good cheer which might reasonably be expected at this hour. Miller, engineer, comes in to say that all the gunners are here for breakfast and will meet us outside in the truck. We finish eating and have time for a leisurely cigarette before going to briefing on the line.

We reach the operations building a few minutes ahead of time and go to the squadron equipment room. It is crowded, and men squeeze back and forth through the door, lugging flying equipment out to waiting trucks. Heavy A-3 bags come crashing over the counter from the supply clerks to the waiting arms of the gunners. I watch our boys. Mussetter, I see, is flashing his gold teeth in the morning. He must be sleeping better these last few days.

The briefing room is rapidly filling as Jack, Fred, and I walk in, handing our passes to the MP at the door. We squeeze in on one of the narrow benches and look around to see who is flying today. But the first glance is at the formation diagram on a giant blackboard to the right front of the room. My name is above the number one cross of the high squadron of the high box. We're the high squadron lead today. I like to fly that spot. Jack and I exchange satisfied glances. Today, we'll be on the very top of the formation. Fred is leading the low squadron of our box.

In the very front and center of this long room, adjacent to our formation diagram, is a huge map of Europe and England. It is now covered with a screen, which hangs all the way to the floor. This map is the focal point of the room. Beneath that screen is a red tape running from our base in England to some point in Germany, which is our target for today. A very few officers know already where we are going—the group S2 and such of his assistants as were needed for the preparation of data for the briefing and pilots, bombardiers, and navigator of the box lead crews, who have already had a special briefing. The rest of us will know when the screen is rolled up. No one is allowed in this room except those actually going on a mission. This is one place you can't come to see your friends off. No one outside this room will know where the mission has gone until we are back at the base or until well after time over target. It is a written and unwritten law: He who knows must not tell, and he who doesn't know must not ask.

The large, rectangular briefing room is crowded with row after row of low benches, right up to the raised platform in front. A narrow aisle runs down the middle of the room to the platform, on which is a little pedestal stand for the briefing officer. Maps, charts, and posters cover the long side walls. The front wall is filled by our giant map and screen and the two large blackboards on either side.

The last stragglers push in, and the room is very crowded. This is an ME (maximum effort), and we are putting up three boxes—thirty-six planes. It is 0355 and a hush gradually falls on the room. Major Garland, who leads the wing today, is in a chair up front. Sitting with him are Colonel Brooks, group executive, and Major Silver, who is briefing officer today. "Pop" Frye, group S2, passes along the crowded aisle to his place in front, chaffing and joking with his boys as he passes. Colonel Brooks walks up to the blackboard and picks up a piece of chalk. There is a shuffling and straining on the benches as all strain to see the figures he puts there: Stations 0530; start engines 0600; taxi 0615; TO 0630. He pauses and looks around with a tantalizing grin to face the hubbub. Slowly and deliberately, he turns and writes the last entry: ETR 1630. A bedlam of groans, whistles, and exclamations well up. Ten hours; this is a deep one!

"Attention."

We pop to attention, and a hush falls. Colonel Bowman, group commander, walks quickly down to his chair in front, turns with a smile, and says quietly, "Be seated, gentlemen."

The briefing officer goes to the blackboard and calls the roll of pilots as they are listed on the formation diagram. The pilots answer for themselves and their crews. All present.

The screen comes up—and there it is! A scarlet line runs upward on the map, turns over the North Sea and stabs the line of the German mainland. It twists and turns between red splotches, which are flak areas, and goes on—goes on until it merges with a huge, heart-shaped splash of red, which is Munich. Two minutes of healthy pandemonium is considered to be in order at this point, and this morning it is indulged to the fullest. Colonel Bowman looks around, smiling like a benevolent schoolmaster who has put a difficult proposition on the board. The faces in the room register every shade of reaction: some tense; some eager; others resigned, or fixed, or nonchalant. I look around and see the old, familiar reactions; Jack slowly shaking his head, eyes half closed; Miller with his shrug and half smile; Mussetter tearing his hair in mock despair. VE, sitting across the aisle, catches my eye. I read the familiar query from his lips, "Think it'll fit?"

Quiet returns and briefing goes on in a businesslike manner.

First the briefing officer: " . . . bomb load, eight 500-lb GP's*, maximum gas load . . ."

Then the weather officer, who speaks with an apologetic air: " . . . surface wind eight to twelve miles per hour, south southeast. Icing level twelve thousand feet. Layer of stratus at three thousand feet. Top nine thousand feet over base and England. Moderate persistent contrails at and above eighteen thousand feet. Cloud cover over target five—to seven-tenths at twelve thousand feet."

Now the briefing navigator, with a time tick and a brief discussion of the route. Then the bombardier, with target pictures on a projector. Lights go out while he pinpoints the target on the screen with a pointer. We see the IP**, the route in, and the point of impact, which is the service installations on a German military airdrome within Munich's cone of fire.

Group S2 Major "Pop" Frye takes over. In a crisp yet genial and fatherly way, he discusses the route in and return. Major Frye is tactful and dwells briefly on the flak situation; in this case, it is self-explanatory. He ends with pertinent PW reminders. "Don't forget your dog tags, your escape kits, and your escape pictures. And don't mention the target!"

The communications and armament follow in quick succession. Colonel Bowman speaks briefly. He has a calm, deliberate, concise voice. His oft-repeated reminders to fly tight formation, to sacrifice the bomb run for nothing, and to be on the lookout for enemy fighters carry conviction.

"Good luck," he says, and briefing is over.

---

*   General Purpose bombs.
**   Initial Point. The exact point of turn onto the bomb run heading.

The crowd mills out. Navigators and bombardiers go to another room for special briefing; gunners go to the ships to install and check their guns; pilots and copilots remain for special briefing.

Pilot's briefing is short. Formation sheets listing position of every crew in formation by number are passed out, together with taxi instruction sheets. Again, the briefing officer gives concise instructions: " . . . assembly over 'Y' buncher. Lead box at ten thousand feet, low at nine thousand feet, high at eleven thousand feet. Flares—lead: green, high: red, low: red-yellow."

Our ritual at the hardstand has become fixed. In our twenty-three previous missions, we have fallen into a familiar routine. The gunners and bombardier have been at the ship almost an hour when the truck brings the rest of us—pilot, copilot, navigator, and radio operator—out from the operations building. It swings around to a stop, and we climb out under the canopy of our craft's right wing. Figures are bustling about in the half-light. James Baker is crouched by his ball-turret just as he was three days ago. Miller is on the left wing, checking the gas caps. I see VE huddled over his sight in the nose. The putt-putt is chattering away, and there is light in the ship. The tail turret is wagging as James Baker makes his final adjustments. Sergeant Hirsch materializes from the darkness and approaches with his customary grave "good morning." The "Form One" is in his hand, and I have a quick look under his flashlight. Everything is ready to go.

Jack deposits his escape kits under the nose, and we swing up through the nose hatch, Hirsch handing in our chutes behind us. "Mac" has already dragged his multitudinous paraphernalia into the nose compartment, and I hear the customary squabbling there. Everything has been checked inside and out, but we hit the high spots again. We spend much time fussing with the little individual arrangements which have become habitual. Ockerman struggles through the hatch with our flak suits and places them, one behind each seat. The helmets are just behind the seats, on top of the chute packs where they can be quickly reached.

"How's the top turret? I ask.

"She's loaded for Bear." And he grins as he strokes the right solenoid. "Bombs are checked," he adds as we squeeze through the narrow catwalk between the two rows of five hundred-pounders. I remember how shocked I was—those huge cylinders in the bomb bay on that first mission.

We find "The Moose" raging like a bull, throwing things around in his radio compartment. He has lost the bolt stud for his .50-caliber flexible. He finds it and subsides. Miller is at the rear door as we step out into the cool darkness.

"Everything's all set," he says, then turns to kid James Baker who is still coddling his ball turret. He's always the last man through, for he is never quite satisfied with his two guns in the steel cocoon.

It is now 0540, so we gather in front of the nose. Jack looks at his kit bag and asks the usual question—"*Who* hasn't an escape kit?"—in a rather weary voice. This time it is Miller who slinks up and pockets the remaining kit, rather sheepishly. We all take a final dig at the cookie bag before Ockerman takes it away for safekeeping. It won't appear again until we're over the Channel on the way back. Hirsch and his boys smoke a final cigarette with us. Now "Mac" gets out his chart and draws us into the light. The ground crew moves away as "Mac" begins his little briefing. He quickly runs over the route, giving the scheduled times at certain points so that, in the event of bailout, everyone will have a general idea where he is and can plan an escape. He answers a few final questions before we're through.

"Anything else?"

"Parson" Baker comes up with his customary reminder: "Anybody using the relief tube, please call me so I can turn the ball turret around."

It seems that, on several occasions, this was neglected, and Baker got a sheet of ice on his turret window—which was scraped off at great inconvenience by Miller, who worked his arm awkwardly through the tiny inspection window. He gets a promise all the way around.

"Time to go. Remember, we've been lucky so far. But look for fighters always. This may be the day." This is my customary warning. We separate, each going to his place in the ship.

The altimeter needle has crawled to nine thousand feet. The blackness we have burrowed through lightens. Abruptly, like a diver reappearing at the surface, our ship tops the cloud layer. We skim along its surface for a moment, brushing up wisps of spray with our wings. Then suddenly it falls away; level, even, as smooth and unbroken as a floor. This is the outer world of emptiness and space. On other days we thread our way through vast columns, under vaulting roofs, or move over wild, desolate moorlands; today we are above an endless gray plain. It stretches on and on. Later it will break; there will be hills and ravines, giant boulders and cliffs. Huge cloud crevasses will appear and below them broken, unrelated patches of the earth will drift. But for hours now we are sealed in this void. Our guides over this trackless waste are unseen and intangible; radio waves, skills we have learned, and plans we have memorized. This space was empty when we came and what trace or trail we leave is not lasting. We may destroy ourselves and our machines in this endless hall, but we can leave no wreckage here. Tomorrow it will be clean.

The needle on the radio compass points "there" and we turn slowly. Far ahead, where our floor is merging from gray to pink, there are heavy black dots. As we watch, they sparkle with red and green lights like strange giant fireflies. They are our lead ships and we turn further to intercept them. Again flares streak upward, pause, then are slowly downward. The dots grow and become planes. Now we join a community. We tuck our plane into its position comfortably above and to the right of our lead ship. The formation grows around us. Planes drift in from all directions and join the cluster, as if drawn by a magnet. By the time the formation is complete we have a cozy, warm feeling. In the formation, as in our own ship, things are settling down for the routine of the long flight. We are making the last few giant circles of the assembly area before starting out in wing formation on the prescribed route to the coast.

Jack flies and I sit back to look over the formation, checking ship numbers against the formation diagram and munching candy from the box on the dashboard. Tail gunner calls to say the second element is in place. I take over, and Jack lights up a cigarette—his last until we are back over the Channel. VE comes through from the bomb bay where he has pulled the pins on our bombs. He scratched Jack behind the ear with the pins, according to custom, and winks as he drops down into the nose compartment.

As our formation crosses the English coast we see the whole armada is falling into line. We are still sealed away by the cloud deck, but radio compass and "Gee box" tell the navigators the moment we are over the edge of land.* This land's end departure is vital to our mission's success. Each wing formation must arrive over the designated point at an exact prearranged time. Thus, hundreds of planes are ordered into one long, continuous train. No one formation can see more than two wings ahead or behind. But the time schedule fits the parts of the train into a definite foreordained pattern. Now we can see the formations immediately ahead and behind us. They seem to float along, like schools of tiny fish.

From our perch on the very top of our wing formation, we look down successively on our lead squadron and our low squadron, slightly behind and below; still further down, upon the lead combat box of three squadrons; and, lower still, the low combat box of three squadrons. It is somewhat like looking down one side of a pyramid from its top, where the steps just below are distinct and of normal size, those lower becoming smaller and more vague in outline; except that this is a gently moving, weaving pyramid, the parts shifting slowly back and forth.

*   *   *

The long climb over the continent begins. We increase power to keep our position, and the altimeter winds slowly. The routine of this flight falls into the usual pattern. Bombardier is on the interphone.

"Bombardier to crew, altitude 11,500. Put on oxygen masks and check in."

One by one the gunners answer, and I call o.k. for pilot and copilot. The top turret is slowly turning as Ockerman takes up his long vigil. Engineer and ball turret are talking on interphone as they make final adjustments before Baker seals himself in his steel ball. Navigator is checking his chart and confirm his ETA for the enemy coast. Tail gunner calls to say that the wingmen and second element have fallen a little behind. He is our eyes to

---

*   Gee Box—An early type of electronic navigation device. The navigator inserted the coordinates of the destination into the gee box, and cursors would intersect to show the destination was found.

the rear as ball turret is eyes below, and top turret above. The engines are smooth and all instruments in the green. Copilot flips the gauges to all tanks in turn, checking fuel. We have "Tokyo" tanks in wingtips.* These we want to drain before we encounter flak. Bombardier calls the gunners for test firing. Soon the ship vibrates and shudders as the turrets fire.

Navigator calls—ETA for IP in target area is twelve thirty; we have three hours. For each man, that time will pass differently. Navigator might as well be in a schoolroom, taking his final exam, except that he is not as comfortable here. He is crouched over his maps and flight plan, computer and pencil in his heavy gloves. Oxygen mask and hose, radio headset and flak suit encumber him. As the clouds break he will vary his constant figuring with checking our position by pilotage, looking at the ground and his map. Bombardier helps with pilotage, checks his bombing data, makes oxygen check every fifteen minutes, is on the alert for fighters with his chin turret. Ball turret, top turret, tail and waist gunners have one job, to know the when and where of enemy fighters and to shoot when they are within range. Now they are calling back and forth checking on our friendly fighter escort. The little friends are with us, sliding impudently back and forth above and below our formations. For pilot and copilot, the time is divided into half-hour intervals of flying and relaxing. When one flies, the other scans the instruments and the sky, observes the formation, and listens on channel "B" (VHF) for bomber-to-bomber communication. From long practice, we automatically switch our jack boxes from VHF to interphone when we change. The man at the controls is always on interphone.

As each man has his job, each has his special weariness, mounting as the hours wear on. A ball turret or a tail turret is cramped and muscles grow sore. The waist gunners are in the coldest, breeziest part of the ship, back in the rattling waist. Even with heated suites and closed windows, a chill mounting in the bones is a special part of their fatigue. Top turret half leans, half stands in his metal and glass cylinder, and turns, turns, turns and he'll hurt to the soles of his feet when he is on the ground again. For pilots it is a gradually developed weariness in arms, and legs, and eyes. Eyes are never still. But for pilots there is a compensation not had by the others. This is flying. It is a break to release the controls and a break to take them

---

*   Tokyo tanks—additional rubberized fuel tanks in the wings of the B-17s, added for extra range.

again. Relax, and you know how tired you are; take over again, and your senses and your reactions push weariness into the background. As for the navigator and bombardier, B-17s—like good bird dogs—have cold noses, and this is no help to them as time wears on.

At 1100 we are deep over Germany. The cloud floor has broken now and large, ragged patches of earth roll beneath us. There is a faint bluish haze, and the terrain below has a mesmeric quality, as if seen through a depth of clear water. It is a quilt work of fields and well-ordered woods, laced with roads. It is remote and unreal as viewed from this great height.

But we are not tourists today, and our concern is in the sky. As we near the target, the growing weariness is thrown off and is replaced by tense expectancy. Fighters are all enemies to the gunners until unmistakable silhouettes or markings are seen. The escort stays well out of range for this reason. The escort is plentiful.

"Bandits in the area," comes in a rather hurried Southern voice, VHF. I relay the message to the crew, then punch "C" button and listen on fighter channel. Somewhere a wing is under attack. The voice of a stricken bomber is calling, hoarse with desperation. He has lost two engines, is turning back and going down, pleading for fighter escort. Again, I warn the gunners.

"Bandits in the area. Keep your eyes peeled, and don't clutter the interphone."

Their voices have a new note as they acknowledge. I feel a strange thrill, a definite quickening, as when I crouched on a deer stand in a southern forest at home, shotgun in hand, and heard the hounds approaching. But in this case, who is the hunter and who is the hunted?

Navigator calls; ETA* for IP is unchanged. Flak pops up three miles or so to the left. Over there, a wing staggers off this island of flak, and one bomber slides down and to the rear, trailing vapor. I look down through a large break. There is a sight for you!

---

*   ETA—Estimated time of arrival.

The Germans can't be sure where we're headed. The present course of the main formations could strike any one of several cities. Every city in this area is putting up a smoke screen. To the left is Hamburg, already covered by a pall of smoke. Further out in front is the beginning of another screen. We can imagine the fear, the confusion, and frantic bustle down there. They hear a mounting, steady thunder and catch glimpses of wing after wing. How do they feel?

Mustangs and Thunderbolts are scurrying all over the sky. Woodcraft White (wing leader) calls VHF; bombing is to be visual. It is 1200. In thirty minutes, we turn on the bomb run. The formations have closed in tighter—as if herded by their bustling watchdogs, the fighters. Flak has been light and sparse until now, but we can expect it at any time from here on. In our ship, flak suits have been put on and helmets stand near to hand. Tokyo drain valves have been closed, gas and oxygen checked, bomb bay doors cracked open and tested. Everything is ready for the few moments that count. We have edged the high squadron closer. Now, as lead ship, we ride just above and to the right of our box lead—almost on top of his wingman.

A red flare goes up from the lead box, the signal for the IP. Our high box falls in line behind the low on the turn. Bombardier calls, "Bomb bay doors open." And Navigator, "Three minutes to target." I see the doors slowly open on the lead ship as we ease down almost level with him, just outside the right wing ship.

How long is a bomb run? Three minutes, three hours or three years it might be. How can we say it? You see the bursts, poisonous black. You feel the ship surge when they are close. You see little holes appear miraculously here and there. In the combat box ahead, just over the target, flak hangs like a heavy black fog, punctuated with bursts and explosions. Another ship peels slowly out and down, away from the formation, with one engine feathered. These things pass quickly and they register fleetingly.

"Thirty seconds to go," from Bombardier.

Three black splashes appear directly in front, like ink spots on a fresh cloth. They dissolve in harmless smoke and whip past our windows. We breathe an acrid odor. A muffled thud like the slamming of a distant door is a close one below. My knees hurt, as they always do in flak, and I wonder if we'll ever drop the bombs. I see beads of sweat on Jack's face, out the corner of my eye. His hand is poised to punch a feathering button if an engine is hit.

The ship gives an unmistakable surge, and we see the cluster of bombs float lazily away from the lead ship. They string out slowly, like the rungs of a ladder unfolding.

"Bombs away," Bombardier sings in the sweetest voice in the world.

The ship seems alive now, relieved of her burden. She prances as we throttle back and settle close above and behind our lead on a shallow, diving turn to the right. Flak bursts follow us around in an eerie stalking sureness, just outside the turn. The low squadron gets a few close bursts, but soon we are free. Ball gunner and radio are jabbering about the bombing—stuff about smoke and explosions below—and the consensus of opinion is that it was a good strike. We settle down on interphone and take up the vigil for fighters.

We are clear of the target and back in wing formation. Several ships are missing from the lead and low boxes. One is missing from our low squadron, tail gunner calls. Cripples float below us, stragglers from many formations. They tag along—one, and sometimes two engines feathered. They fall behind gradually, tagging one formation as long as possible then falling back to the next, fighting to save altitude and stay with friends. To the right, a lone bomber is going down steadily. A fighter swoops down and gives it escort until, finally, chutes blossom below her. She wheels over slowly and deliberately then spins.

In our own ship, flak damage is reported in the radio room, on the tail surfaces, and wings. We relax a bit, for there is no indication of serious damage. Bombardier has received OK on all stations on his check when we cleared the flak.

* * *

We are at nine thousand feet over the Channel. After seven hours and better on oxygen, we can at last tear the masks away and breathe naturally.

It is sheer joy and unspeakable relief. No other cigarette can compare in taste and life-giving quality to this first one we light here in comparative safety after eight hours of tenseness. The crew remains at stations as we near the English coast, and our formation slips in under the broken cloud deck at less than two thousand feet. Formation flying is tricky and difficult now. Prop wash can be serious at this low altitude, and the air is rough and bumpy. Sometimes this last half hour over England is toughest of all for the pilots, who are dead tired at this point.

I look down on the familiar green countryside. Only weeks ago, we were at Bovington, waiting shipment to a combat group. How we watched these returning formations, counted stragglers, noted the gaps in formations. Long-sought landmarks roll beneath us, and soon we see the familiar pall of smoke, which hangs over the great mills at Corby. Mechanically, instinctively, Jack and I go over the before-landing operations. At long last, we are peeling off in formation; heading in on the final approach; are landing and rolling to a gradual shop; are taxiing around the perimeter; are following the welcome hand signals of Sergeant Hirsch as he directs us to our parking place on the hardstand. At last we have finished, and the props whirl to a stop.

There are chores at the end as well as the beginning. Stiffly, dazedly, we gather our equipment—chutes, Mae Wests, oxygen masks, heated suits, guns—and stack them on the truck that has swung into the hardstand. Hirsch and his boys are around us, hearty and sincere, glad we are back. With the gunners, they swarm over the ship, counting flak holes and checking damage. I sign the Form One and talk briefly with Hirsch about the ship. The boys are assembling last-minute articles. There is always a search for a missing firing pin, a bolt stud, or an escape kit. A squabble and a showdown, and someone comes up sheepishly with the missing articles. They babble about the mission and the flak and examine the holes in the ship. Damage is not very heavy, and she will be flyable tomorrow. Just now, that is a matter of small interest to us. We finally pile in the truck and are off to interrogation.

The main briefing room is as much a hubbub now as it was before briefing this morning. The Intelligence officers have their tables set up there, and crews are streaming in for interrogation. Red Cross girls are flitting back and forth with pitchers of strong black coffee; cakes and cups are on each table. We sit down to our coffee and cake and give our news to Captain Red, our interrogator. His questions cover flak, enemy fighters, our own escort, time, altitude, and place of any usual observations. Mac thumbs his long sheet and supplies most of the information. I look around through the blue haze of cigarette smoke and see men in all shades of relaxation after a grueling mission. The hum of voices has a tenseness, an excitement running through it. Questions are being answered with much gesturing and brandishing of coffee cups. Eventually, we are finished with our last gulps of coffee; the mission is over.

It is 1900, late afternoon, and I'm back on the bunk after a hot shower and a drink and dinner at the club with Opie and Grumman. Now I begin to know how tired I am. It was sixteen hours ago that we woke here and dressed for this day's work. Since that time, we have been into an unreal world. Facts cannot tell the story. We have flown some seventeen hundred miles. We have been in the air well over ten hours and have burned two thousand gallons of gasoline. We have dropped four thousand pounds of explosives upon an installation which to us was the target—a specific place on the map of Germany, a picture in a bombsight. We have been less than a thousandth part of a gigantic machine, composed of men and machines, which has done its work for the day and now is at rest.

Some who woke with us this morning are hiding in the woods in Germany; others are prisoners standing before German intelligence officers. Some are dead. We moved through a gigantic shifting panorama, out on the rim of life. Death was painted there in deceiving forms—in empty puffs of smoke, in a single splash of orange where a plane exploded, and in twisting silver leaves drifting slowly earthward. Now all that remains are fleeting images on the mind and complete weariness of the body.

With a pencil, I mark the twenty-fourth tally on the right leg of a nameless pinup girl from *Yank*. She hangs on the wall by my bed where she was left by the former occupant. Her left leg has twelve tallies.

Weather looks bad, and it is a stand-down for tomorrow. Blackout curtains are a great institution born of war, and we'll use them far into the morning.

CHAPTER EIGHT

BETWEEN TIMES

8-1 Boxers—Boxing lessons from Jack Dempsey, world heavyweight boxing champion and U.S. Navy officer (401st Bomb Group Association Album, 1948).

8-2 Party Time—Party night at the 401st Officer's Mess (401st Bomb Group Association Album, 1948).

8-3 Waiting for friends to return from a bombing mission—Lt. F. M. Taylor, Greenville, South Carolina. (Flight training with Lt. J. F. Risher); Lt. W. A. Roesky, Milford, Michigan; Lt. V. B. Coyne, Robinson, Illinois.

Source: 401st Bomb Group Association Photograph
Taken by J. F. Risher, Jr. (401st Bomb Group)

8-4 Furry friends—Pets of all descriptions were common in U.S. Army Air Force units. Animals provide comfort and distraction from combat stress (401st Bomb Group Album, 1948).

8-5 Weldon Chapel—Stained glass windows in the eight-hundred-year-old Weldon Chapel near Kettering, England. Window panels showing U.S. and U.K. flags and B-17s flying through clouds were dedicated to the church as a gift from the 401st Bomb Group, Deenthorpe, England.

Photos taken by J. F. Risher III in 1993.

VIII. BETWEEN TIMES

The experiences of combat cannot be fully appreciated from the vantage point of normal living. They involve so much more than shooting and being shot at, and are so much the climax of a gradual, systematic training whereby the individual's outlook has been adjusted to its ordeal. Common sense and ordinary imagination tell us that minds and nerves are under unusual stresses. Well-intended writers, therefore, have sometimes been guilty of overdramatizing the feelings and actions and words of men before, during, and after combat. Normal men do feel intensely and vividly, but fortunately, their entire plane of feeling has been elevated, quickened, and made ready. Thus, the average tenor of existence is much nearer ordinary living than might seem likely.

Walking into a barracks where officers or men spent the evening before a combat mission, one might have thought he was in some barracks of a training base in the United States. Some would have been reading, some talking or writing letters, others sleeping. Undoubtedly, a more or less profane card game would have been in progress. There would have been no hushed, last-minute confidences; no leaving of notes or trinkets to be delivered, just in case; and there would have been very few just-before-the-battle letters among those written. Someone would have strolled out to sniff the weather. If it looked definitely like a "scrubbed" mission, the card game would have gone on into the night. If it looked as if an early mission was probable, someone would have complained about the lights soon. Probably, they would have gone out at an early hour. There would have been talking and chuckling back and forth. Soon only snores and the twisting and turning of restless sleepers would have broken the silence.

This does not imply that the inward feelings were always relaxed. It was simply that there was no adequate, acceptable way of dealing with them except to control them. This life had surrounded you and engulfed you. The tautness and tenseness before a mission was a part of it, just as much as the glorious feeling of weariness and accomplishment, which came at the end. There were no mock heroics, no gesturing. Happily, normal, healthy men are able to adapt themselves to almost any job, or life in any conceivable situation, with a certain degree of stoicism.

When men returned to a barracks or squadron area after a grueling mission, and there were empty bunks and missing friends, there were no silly, coined phrases to hide the obvious facts. We did not tacitly bar the mentioning of them. Whether by common understanding or common sense, there was no long-drawn lamenting; but there was often frank discussion. Three were seen to bail out, and there was a good chance they were all POWs or the ship went down in flames, and it did not look too good for them. If they were close friends, it hurt very much. If they were not, it may not have registered particularly.

There were no downcast eyes or averted glances at the mention of certain names. There was natural regret and deep feeling often. But even this was sheathed over, and dulled, and pushed into the background by the pace of the existence. If a friend or acquaintance was lost three missions ago, it might have been three years in normal life. The reaction was what might reasonably have been expected of normal human beings—but humans who had gradually, unknowingly become acclimated to an intensified existence.

When missions came regularly, there was no question about the employment of spare time. Sleeping ("sacking") was a favorite diversion. It took time to recover energy lost in an eight—or ten-hour mission, and most men found a couple of days lounging on the bunk quite in order when it was possible. Those men who could not sleep before a mission were often able to make up for it during those days when no mission was imminent. And then there were times when we flew two and three, and sometimes more, missions in daily succession. When such a grind was followed by a few days on the ground, most men used the time off to break even on sleep and rest. They were content to sit around in barracks reading or writing letters, or to assume the horizontal and sleep. As a rule, we stayed on the base between the regular forty-eight-hour passes, which normally came every two weeks. Except during June and early July, when there were no passes for combat crews.

*   *   *

There were certain duties on the ground. School, gunnery trainer, ditching and bailout drills, and critiques—necessary training, and enough to keep the men from becoming bored if the weather grounded us for any long period. The policy was to accomplish the amount of training thought necessary and otherwise to give the combat crews a reasonable amount of free time. We flew frequent practice missions. It was a pleasant change from flying missions over enemy territory, burdened with flak suits and oxygen masks, to fly at low altitude over England. In our crew these flights furnished a chance for each of us to move around the ship and see how the other fellow lived. Radio and ball turret might navigate, engineer fly as copilot, and copilot take over the top turret. In due time, everyone flew the ship while pilot or copilot looked on. All of us dropped at least one practice bomb, for VE usually saved the last of his practice bombs for somebody else.

It is a well-known fact that American soldiers the world over had a propensity for collecting pets—children and animals alike. Pets of various descriptions were numerous on bomber bases, many of them being handed down through several generations of crews. Our crew ran true to form. Shortly after we arrived in the squadron one of the veteran crews finished a tour of missions. This crew had a little monkey, "Jocko" by name. Our sergeants arranged to buy him, so we all chipped in to raise the purchase price of five pounds. Harry Baker and Bob Ockerman built a little house for Jocko and placed it just behind their long tin barracks. Any late afternoon would find a cluster of officers and enlisted men standing around watching the antics of Jocko. He was playful but unpredictable in his moods. One time, he sidles up to a bystander, very placating in manner, expecting some little treat. Again, he might lunge unexpectedly at one of his audience and gum furiously at his cuffs. He made a great pretense of biting, though he never actually bit anyone. He threw frequent tantrums. He would scramble up the corner of the barracks and sit on the roof, scowling and jabbering at the crowd below. Jocko was so erratic and unpredictable in his behavior that we all said he had a solid case of combat fatigue.

Then there was Gertrude. Frank and Jack paid ten pounds for a very beautiful cocker spaniel puppy and brought her to our barracks.

Poor old Frank learned a few things quickly. Kelly had kept a puppy in barracks until it suddenly became ill and died. We all, therefore, knew some of the more unpleasant aspects of having one in barracks when Gertrude came along. Her reception was cool at first. But Frank was very faithful and devoted to her. The moment someone yelled bloody murder

and cut loose with a string of profanity directed at all dogs in general,
Frank would pick up his little shovel, scoop up some ashes, and proceed
directly to the trouble spot. Sometimes Gertrude brought things to a near
crisis with her indiscriminate behavior. Jangled nerves and short tempers
were often taxed. But Gertrude was a rambler by nature; she explored our
long barracks from end to end, and she played no favorites. If a fellow was
at the exploding point when Frank piled the ashes beside his bunk, he had
only to wait a while, and he could laugh at someone else. In a matter of a
few days, Gertrude's innate charm and Frank's suave handling of delicate
situations had won us over. Gertrude was there to stay. The little ash hills
became a common and unnoticed part of our floor. Soon everyone brought
something from the mess hall for Gertrude; if ever a puppy was raised on
an irregular diet, this one was. Frank was like a mother trying to rear a
baby with the "in-laws" or grandparents. Gertrude lived with a houseful of
people who were determined to spoil her to death.

Each barracks over there became somewhat of an informal club. Not
overlooking the Group Officers Club—with the occasional group parties,
the bar, and the mighty poker games which sometimes took place there—the
barracks was the hub of our life between missions. There in barracks were
the more terrific bull sessions and the frequent horseplay. There were the
closest associations. Officers and enlisted men visited each other often, and
a general camaraderie existed. In these visits back and forth, we fortified
the bonds between us.

On a dull night of bad weather, anything might happen in barracks.
One night some of us were gathered around our little peat stove and
Kelly's broken-down toaster. Kelly's toast only whetted appetites and talk
inevitably turned to food. Someone suggested that fried chicken would
go well at this point. The idea passed for a while but came up again after
the bottle of Scotch had circulated once more. Suddenly, VE, Kelly, and
Wilson's tail gunner disappeared. In fifteen minutes they were back and a
big sack was swinging over VE's shoulder. Out of that sack he pulled five
dressed chickens. He also produces flour, salt, and other necessary items. In
a welter of confusion, stumbling and bumping back and forth, the fire was
built up, our shaving pails scrubbed out, and chicken a' la unknown was
on the way. Chief cook (Lieutenant Brown) and assistant (Sergeant Bailey)
directed operations, and out of all the confusion came the best chicken any
of us ever ate.

We had our own private buzz-bomb warfare too. Frank started this innocently enough one night when he made a paper airplane, touched it with lighter fluid and a match, and sent it streaming fire to VE's bunk just across the barracks. That opened a mighty bombardment back and forth which went on for weeks, steadily increasing in scope and intensity. The end came one night after a "group party" at the officers' club. Others had become involved in the big fracas and, on the final night, when the barracks almost burned down, VE and "Shorty" were at war. Buzz bombs flew thick and fast between their bunks. In a furious ten-minute battle, they grew from tiny paper darts with a drop of lighter fluid ignited on the end to a wad of newspaper, streaming fire. At the climax, Shorty introduced V2 in the form of a wad of *London Times*, which seemed to explode as it struck Brown's bunk. It landed in a little puddle of lighter fluid, and in a matter of seconds, the battlers and the spectators were stamping around, putting out a very promising blaze. VE had lost a pair of dress shoes, a mattress, and a pair of trousers, and the buzz-bomb warfare was over. A couple of shots from his .45 into the roof after the lights were out served as an official salvo to mark the end of hostilities.

*   *   *

A forty-eight-hour pass was a two-day haven of safety and freedom for men who were otherwise always on call for danger. It was a short time during which they knew they were out of the war. For this reason passes were rather vivid experiences, even though occasionally they were spent in a more sane manner than might be thought.

For crews based in our area, London was the logical spot for a pass. Perhaps all of us, no matter what our interests, whether of a cultural nature or of a more prosaic sort, left London for the last time feeling that we had not by any means exhausted all possibilities. This takes into consideration the fact that each one in his own way spent every leave as though it were his last, which was a logical attitude under the circumstances.

This broad, sprawling city enveloped us for these short periods. Its ancient yet ageless appearance registered on all though London was full of war, it carried to me, and I think too many others, a suggestion of being remote and impervious to it. Its aged landmarks, it's very air, breathed a suggestion that this thing which now filled our lives was only a passing, though crucial, moment in the history of the ages. Despite blitz and buzz bombs, there were a hundred quiet squares where there was no sign or evidence or suggestion of war.

And there was Piccadilly Circus. There are probably two reasons why Piccadilly was the hub of our leaves. Piccadilly Circus was the one landmark, aside from Westminster Abbey, which every American schoolboy knew; and Piccadilly Circus, in and around its hub, contained all the essential elements of a successful leave. Hotels, theaters, churches, bars and pubs, and women were in that vicinity. A man could consult his taste and spend his leave to his own satisfaction, having all his needs close at hand. For our crew, there was a small hotel—the Winston, off Piccadilly—which was a rallying point.

The "Regency Palace" Hotel was a center for a lot of things. This was the best place to go if you were looking for a friend from another base who might be in town. This was where you often learned who had been shot down, who had finished, or how many missions a friend had.

Buzz bombs figured in our visits to London. There were few of us who did not, sooner or later, see this weird thing hurtling along overhead, hear the silence after the engine cut, and feel the explosion which followed, perhaps half a dozen blocks away. Combat men visiting London (except those who had close misses) seemed not to be disturbed by the buzz bombs. Perhaps the nature of our daily work away from London was such that we could more easily adopt the philosophy that "London was so big, and we were so small." I visited London a number of times while flying missions and heard the bombs on every trip. During this time, the buzz bomb was—from my personal standpoint—more a curiosity than a source of possible danger. But on my last visit, after I had completed my missions and was waiting shipment home, the effect was somewhat different. I should confess that I did not enjoy this pass. I left London for the last time with a very keen appreciation of what a trial these things were to Londoners who were going about in the ways of ordinary living under them. Somehow it had been easier when my psychology and outlook were gauged to flying combat missions.

Among those who had perilously close calls with the buzz bomb was an officer from our squadron. He was in London on a leave—his last there—and was sitting in a little park with a girl. The sirens moaned, but they continued their engaging conversation on the bench. Before they were aware of it, a buzz bomb was overhead—was cutting power and nosing downward. It landed squarely in the center of the duck pond in the middle of the park. My friend picked himself and his girl up from the ground. They were covered with mud and duck feathers, were chastened and shaken; and my friend, at least, was filled with a strong desire to get out of London. Thereafter, he remained on our base or went on local excursions when he had a pass. He continually badgered this or that hardy soul who was venturing to London with requests for purchases at the Post Exchange there. He had seen enough.

*   *   *

It would be gratifying if we could say that officers and men spent much of their time discussing the issues of war and the peace to follow; if we could say that their conversations revealed a burning zeal and an ever present sense of high moral purpose; that they were absorbed in visions of the brave new world to come. But in so far as one participant was able to observe, this was not true. On the whole, combat men and officers talked most often about things that concerned them primarily or immediately—missions, home, wives, and families, the current crop of rumors. They talked about religion infrequently and seldom, very seldom, about death.

This does not necessarily imply that our combat soldiers and officers were indifferent to the issues of the war—that they took this as just another job that must be done—or that they were on the whole callous to the thoughts of religion. It simply bears out what now seems to be a fact; namely, that the American male is not by nature a zealous crusader, that he is not given to emoting about the cause for which he fights or the faith which sustains him in the fight.

Certainly, there were very few men who had not thought carefully in their own minds of the position they found themselves in—this curious situation wherein they went out to risk their lives, came back to relative security, then went out again, day after day, until they had been put out of action or had accomplished an allotted contribution to a vast enterprise; few who had not decided simply for themselves that it was necessary and right and that they could and did take a pride in it. And religion—or more pointedly perhaps, faith in God—was present in our lives more significantly than ever before. A man who has completed a tour of combat missions has had a religious experience, whether he tells you about it or not. These things were tacitly understood and accepted among us. But they were largely left out of conversations and associations.

It is a fact, of course, that all men who had a nucleus of religious faith, drew upon it for spiritual strength in the stress of combat, and in so doing they added to that faith, though this may not have been evident by anything they said. I feel sure that many men who saw armed combat in this war have had something definite added to their religious faith and convictions, something which will serve them in later years, and serve them all the better because it was tested under fire. There is no doubt that simple faith in God and prayer sustained men in all kinds of combat, men who had never before realized what a powerful spiritual brace lay within their reach.

Anyone who completed a tour of combat missions had occasion to review and consolidate his thoughts about death. The general attitude was surprisingly normal, and the seeming indifference came, probably, from the inability of healthy young men to visualize themselves as dead. I know that this is true, if observation of others and personal experience are evidence. It was a constant surprise to realize that, on the whole, I and all those around me were living this unusual existence in very much the normal, everyday frame of mind, even though our whole plane of thinking and feeling *had been* adjusted to an unusual level, as most of us were to discover during the few months after return home from combat.

But, most individuals somewhere along in their tour of missions momentarily lost this perhaps exaggerated confidence in their own invulnerability. Everyone, somewhere in the long procession of missions found himself the victim of raw nerves and a temporary physical let-down; found himself temporarily despondent and fearful of the next mission. Most times he might say to himself, "Tomorrow I go on my sixteenth mission—(or twelfth or twentieth)." But sometimes he would say within himself but not say it aloud: "Tomorrow, I may die. Tomorrow, I am going on a hazardous journey, the like of which is unheard of in an ordinary, sane world. I will be exposed to many dangers for hours on end. Many enemies, on the ground and in the air, will be coldly and deliberately trying to shoot me out of the sky. This has been going on for some time. I cannot be lucky always." And then he would think, perhaps, of the other healthy extroverts he had known, who had gone out for missions with all the confidence he normally had, and who had not come back. He would think of his friend who had gone down the other day; who had occupied the bunk across the barracks, and who had three more to go when his luck ran out. And these thoughts would not cheer him any.

But, granted that much of the time a man was buoyed up by some innate confidence and that sometimes he was plainly afraid, there is another consideration more interesting.

One thing we lose, at least temporarily, and that is our *respect for death* as the culmination of human life. Death is cheapened in combat. It is no longer the tragic or beautiful thing it is in a normal world. It is a casual, commonplace thing, however regrettable.

*   *   *

When I was a boy, there was one spot in the countryside around my home which was strangely marked. Near my home was a little country church, long deserted. Once, years before my time, it had been the place of worship and the community rendezvous and gathering spot for most of the people who lived in that section. They came and sat on the hard, straight benches and listened to the long, sonorous sermons of many a fire-baiting preacher. They stood around under the trees after the services and talked, the women in a cluster by the front steps, the men gathered to one side under a giant oak. The air was filled with the sound of slow, unhurried voices and the smell of tobacco from strong pipes. And then, one by one, the family groups collected and wagons and buggies moved out from the grove of trees and went their separate ways. This went on for years. Life was unhurried among these people, and unspectacular.

But even here the collision of separate human destinies and desires could be tragic, and was. One Sunday morning after church the congregation stood around as usual and talked in leisurely fashion. But two men stood off to one side, under a small oak, and talked, at first in quiet tones, and then heatedly. One pistol shot rang out and the drifting tobacco smoke took on a pungent smell. John Edwards had killed Ed Haley, there under the little oak, and this place was forever changed.

The killing was many years old when I first knew of it but the place was marked in memory. The church, long since deserted, stood as a forlorn and ghostly skeleton, half hidden in the tall grove. The colored folk avoided the spot and it was seldom that anyone had occasion to go near it. It stood, and still stands, in that community as a symbol of the tragedy of unnatural, violent death.

There in England, on occasional summer afternoons when some of us who were not flying the mission lay in the sun outside our barracks and dozed or talked, I thought of my first and only visit to that little church. I remembered how strangely fascinated I was by the thoughts which arose when I stood under the tree which marked the spot *of this* old tragedy. "He fell right under that oak," my uncle had said as we walked though the old churchyard on the way to one of his fields, "and he was dead before they picked him up." He had pointed to a sizeable tree standing some ten yards or so from the crumbling walls of the old building. This tree had been a mere scrub twenty years ago when Ed Haley died under it. Twenty long, slow, monotonous years had slid by this place since a man had died prematurely here. The tree had grown, the building had crumbled, the witnesses of the tragedy had long since scattered. And yet, had he not died violently because of some entwining of human destinies unknown to me and forgotten now by most of those who knew, he would have been a middle-aged man: a robust, hearty, plain-living man typical of this part of the country.

Twenty winters and twenty summers had passed this place. Breezes had rustled the leaves of the tree in the summer, year after year, and winds had rattled its branches in winter; and all the long years it had grown, slowly but inevitably, while a man who should have been alive today, and in his prime, had long since dissolved into nothing. He had died obscurely but his death had been marked as far as his life would have reached. This spot, this very spot, was the place where in a single moment of violence one life had been ended, and others had been forever altered and transposed within their spheres. Whether the man had died by his own misguided actions or those of his killer, whether or not his killing had been justified by the laws of the land, was now of no consequence. A fundamental fact of human existence, the final and irrevocable fact, had been enacted here.

But in this English countryside, peaceful though it seemed, we were living on a plane which did not encourage or allow us to think of death in that way. For the time being, at least, it must be viewed coldly and logically. It was simply a rate of attrition in an unusual sort of enterprise. For the time being, an exploding bomber could not and would not be thought of as the tragic death of ten young men, but as part of an inevitable loss percentage. Though a tractor ticked away on a distant hillside and the air was filled with the universally peaceful smells of the country, empty bunks must be thought of as available bunks, and personal effects of men shot down, as military baggage for shipment. The change had not been forced; it was inevitable.

*   *   *

A day on the ground while the group was away gave one a keen perception of the length of an average mission.

You got up at 0900 and dressed leisurely for a late breakfast in the snack bar of the combat mess. As you dressed, you looked around at the empty bunks of those who had gone on the mission. Those bunks had been empty since 0200—seven hours. You dimly remembered the lights being on, hearing shuffling and moving as your barracks mates dressed. At the mess hall, you learned that takeoff was at 0600. They had been in the air three hours and probably were still boring toward the target.

You finished breakfast and strolled down to the gunnery trainer where the sergeants of your crew were scheduled for an hour of training. On the way back, you stopped by the orderly room and picked up your mail, and at the barracks, you read your letters and wrote a couple. It was 1230 and time for lunch. The mission had been in the air six and one-half hours now. At the mess hall, a friend from S2 told you they were due back at 1530 (he could tell you now, for they were over the target an hour ago). You finished lunch and went over to the crew library for an hour and better of reading. You later stopped by the photo shop on your way to barracks. At barracks, you read *Stars and Stripes* then lounged and talked till 1500. This was the ninth hour.

Now all movement seemed drawn irresistibly toward the line. Your bike joined the steady flow of jeeps and bicycles down the highway toward the field. At the far end of the field, near the end of the landing runway and beside the highway, a cluster *was* gathering, soldiers and civilians.

Base operations building, on the edge of the field, was flanked by jeeps, command cars, trucks, and bicycles; and a number of officers and men were lounging outside, waiting. Inside, there was a bustle as S2 officers prepared their tables for interrogation of crews. A group of officers were gathered on the balcony of the control tower, and all along the perimeter track, ground crews were waiting at their hardstands. The sky was streaked with formations headed for home bases. Bomber formations drifted along with a muted roar, while fighters snarled past them, moving like birds before a storm.

Then our own formations came over—two boxes—and all heads were lifted to count the total. Four were missing, but perhaps some were camera ships and landed earlier after leaving formation at the coast. It later developed that only one of the missing was lost, shot down over the target. We watched them as they peeled off and landed and as they taxied around the perimeter. Tired crews waved to friends in front of the buildings, and we waved back as the familiar planes moved past.

The first crews tumbled off the trucks in front of operations, and you saw how tired they were, how grimy and lined their faces. You—relaxed after a long sleep and quiet day—were struck with the tense excitability in their voices, their generally high-pitched demeanor. They were bone tired and drunk with their own adrenalin. You remembered your long, lazy day. During all this time, and for hours before, they had been in the air. For longer than a normal working day, they had sat in their seats or crouched in their turrets, without relief or rest or pause from concentration.

My crew had occasion to remember vividly one of those days on the ground. One afternoon, early in June, we were out on the skeet range when the group returned from the day's mission. Wilson and his crew had gone on this one, and we were sweating them out for their twenty-sixth mission. Four more after this one, and they would finish their tour. They had taken their share of rough going. The first box came over with all ships and peeled off for landing; then the second. The third box came over with *three* ships missing. We finished our round of skeet and hurried over to the briefing rooms where interrogation was going on. There we heard the news. Three ships were shot down by fighters, and Wilson's was one of them. We didn't want to believe it. This near the end, and after so much!

We returned to the empty barracks. There were their beds, their clothes, their personal belongings. A pair of pajamas hung over the foot of a bed where they had been hastily thrown in the early morning. *Whistle Stop* lay on Connery's table. He had been reading it the night before and had stopped at page 191. There was old Kelly's little toaster, with half a loaf of bread beside it. He had always stopped by the mess hall on his way to the barracks at night and wheedled some bread and butter. They had been strangers a month ago but now were brothers missing.

They had twenty-six, and we had six. Weather was bad for several days, and we were grounded. This was, beyond doubt, the low point of our morale as a combat crew. The bitter news of Wilson and crew coincided with the transfer of Frank Ricks to another crew, previously recounted.

Within a week, the weather cleared. New crews moved in. We remembered that first afternoon when we had come there. We resumed our schedule of missions.

CHAPTER NINE

MEN AND PLANES

9-1-401st Group Jackets.

9-2 Home James—was flown seventeen missions by the Risher crew until a disaster on the ground.

(401st Bomb Group Association)

9-3 Hard Seventeen—was flown to Munich and Peenemunde.

(401st Bomb Group Association)

9-4 Rosie's Sweat Box
42-97872
Photo Taken: 30 May 1944

Source: 401st BG Association Collection

Flown on July 25, 1944, St. Lo Mission—almost blown out of the sky.

9-5 Miss "B" Haven
42-31863
Photo Taken: 30 May 1944

Photo Courtesy of National Archives #65642-B

#42-97395 Chute the Works
Photo Taken: 30 Jan 1945

Photo Courtesy of National Archives #10313

9-6 Chute the Works—Flown on the last Risher crew mission (#32) to Weimar, Germany, August 24, 1944.

IX. MEN AND PLANES

It is the pilot who knows, feels, and contends with the vagaries and idiosyncrasies of planes; who finds as much difference between one type of plane and another as that between two human personalities; and who must constantly adjust and temper his flying technique and his touch on the controls to the particular type of plane he is flying at the moment. The pilot finds that, no matter how large or small the plane, it is a live thing in his hands, a creature with a power of response, a discriminating sense of touch, and a will of its own.

What we say here concerns the average GI pilot—the fellow who was good enough; who was sometimes more than good, in fact; and who at times knew within himself that he was just fair. This fellow may not even have thought seriously of flying military planes before the war, and never would have, had there been no war. He worked himself into the air force because he thought it was a pretty good way to serve, and even when he was flying himself to the verge of exhaustion in combat or training, he could occasionally wake up to a huge satisfaction at the thought that he was flying a B-17, a P-51, a P-38, or a B-29. We are talking about the man who was engaged during the two or three years of his wartime experience in one of the most interesting and demanding types of work open to men; who, perhaps, could not fully appreciate his work or know what it meant to him at the time; and now, having returned to civilian life and other pursuits, is beginning to realize that, after all, his military flying was a pretty wonderful experience.

The pilot has often been pictured as a kid dressed in uniform, with crumpled cap pushed back on his head, cigarette in mouth, and hands in pocket—the very antithesis of what an officer should be in appearance and bearing. This, of course, is a fairly accurate picture of a considerable number of the officers who flew our combat planes in this war. Substitute a pair of moccasins for the regulation shoes and throw in an off-color necktie or shirt and the picture will be a bona fide reproduction. Needless to say, this conception certainly did not apply to all, or even most, pilots and other rated officers, but it illustrates the point that flying officers generally were rather lax in their conception of ground duties and decorum, routine or nonflying responsibilities.

The amazing thing, the constant point of wonder, was that these kids who appeared so absolutely irresponsible on the ground would be transformed into precise, exacting, painstaking, and thoroughly conscientious and zealous technicians the moment they were seated in the cockpit of an airplane. Many pilots who took very lightly their duties and responsibilities as officers on the ground goaded themselves to continuous improvement in their flying techniques. Officers who viewed other duties with extreme nonchalance prided themselves on perfection and smoothness in flying. We did not fully realize it, but it was innate respect for the art of flying and for the planes we flew which was responsible for this fact.

*   *   *

There probably has never been a more unique relationship between teacher and pupil than that which existed between the flying instructor and the cadet or pilot he was instructing. From primary all the way through flying school, and wherever afterward two men were seated in an airplane as instructor and student, there was a touch-and-go contact between personalities not to be found elsewhere. Probably every air force pilot remembers his primary instructor more vividly than any other person he was ever associated with in his flying career; and it was because it was with this man that he first encountered this peculiar relationship. It is probable also that every pilot carried over into his later flying habits most of the principles or techniques taught him by his first instructor. I recall, for example, that my primary instructor (a beautiful soul by name of Welsh, from Uvalde, Texas), was adamant when it came to low, dragging approaches for landing. He insisted that his students learn to gauge distance and altitude so that a landing could be made in the first third of the field without a last minute burst of power and a dragging approach to reach the edge of the field. He preferred a landing slightly long on the runway to one dropped in on the very edge after a low approach. In all my flying since primary, in various types of ships, my tendency has been to err, if at all, in favor of the high approach. In heavy ships, I have sometimes had to cut off all power short of the edge of the field in order to land properly, but seldom have I had to drag the ship in after undershooting the field.

By pride of profession, we do not mean that bombastic line of bull usually associated with the "hot pilot." This was something very definitely frowned upon by most flyers, and any pilot found giving forth with glowing tales of his own exploits, or exaggerating the hazards or the difficulties of flying in the presence of the uninitiated, was apt to get a sound ribbing by his fellows. The real pride of profession was the individual pilot's inward satisfaction when he knew that he was doing a good job of flying, and his disappointment and self-reproach when he knew that his flying was sloppy or uncoordinated. It was the pride and the self-reproach of the athlete. All pilots have been, at one time or another, afraid of airplanes—most especially when they have not been flying regularly; and at other times, have exulted in their mastery over them.

In flying, pride of profession was evident where two strangers worked together at their specialty. It was not evident in what was said; on the contrary, most pilots studiously avoided, when flying with a stranger, giving any appearance of anxiety or concern over the way the other man was handling the plane, except in the case of instructor and student. But when two rated, experienced pilots flew together, you may be sure that the man handling the plane was very conscious of his flying and that the other was taking silent and unconsciously critical note of his technique. The observer saw when a hundred feet was lost in a turn; he saw when the airspeed moved up and down on instrument flying, and when the heading weaved back and forth; he noted a sloppy pattern for landing. His eyes, roving idly and casually over the instrument panel, took in all the details which denoted smooth and precise, or sloppy and erratic flying. And the man who was flying took an inward satisfaction at a smooth landing, or felt lamely apologetic at a bumpy one.

Flying—and therefore, the airplane—was the best and surest test of a pilot's physical and mental well-being. Every pilot experienced slumps and peaks in his flying efficiency, and invariably, he found that it was tied in with his state of health or frame of mind at the moment. The time has long since passed when it was thought that flying was a profession for a select few men of exceptional physical qualifications, and we know now that the majority of adults are physically qualified to fly and that, of this majority, a considerable number are capable of flying the military type of aircraft. But those of us who flew Air Corps and navy tactical airplanes knew that with any individual, flying efficiency fluctuated, and that a man who prided himself in this profession and who expected to continue in it for a reasonable length of time must recognize it for what it is: an exacting physical and mental test.

All flying crew members learned in time to sense and evaluate pilot techniques. In all combat, lives depend upon leadership, and nowhere was this more literally true than on the crew of a combat airplane. Here the leader not only coordinated the efforts of the others, but the fate of all hung every day on his mind and his reflexes, his judgment, and his reactions to emergencies. We do not intend to glorify the pilot here, but simply to state a condition that thousands of very ordinary young men met through proper training, without, perhaps, being aware of its significance.

All crew members could sense a good or bad approach for landing, a smooth or ragged takeoff, and good or poor formation flying. All could tell from the feel and sound of the airplane whether everything was normal or trouble was being experienced.

For all the members of a combat crew, the particular plane they flew was the ultimate perfection in flying machines. Much good-natured (and some heated) exchanges went on between pilots, and other crew members, of various types of ships as to the respective merits of the planes in question.

Beyond question it was a P-51 (Mustang) or P-38 (Lightning) pilot who dubbed the P-47 (commonly known as the Thunderbolt) as "A monstrous crescendo of noise, usually accompanied by a flash of lightning, signifying nothing." And it was a B-17 pilot or crew member who defined the B-24 as "The Flying Box Car" and "The Flying Windmill." In the grim humor of combat, B-17 men laughingly said that when B-24s were on a mission with them, they had the best possible escort; the B-17s, they said, scrawled a sign on their fuselages, pointing in the general direction of the B-24 formations and reading "B-24s over there" for the benefit of German fighter pilots.

*   *   *

In the early days of the Eighth Air Force, certain plane names were household words. "Southern Comfort," "Memphis Belle," and "Tar Baby" are among the illustrious ladies of the pioneer days who were known to us all. In those days when they were numbered in tens and hundreds, rather than in thousands, planes and crews alike stood out individually. In the last two years of the European War, however, the Eighth Air Force grew from a small task force into a vast enterprise involving scores of air bases and thousands of planes. Naturally and rightfully, the sense of individuality was lost. Planes became numbers again, so far as the general view is concerned. Only by intimate study do we know how important a plane was to the men who flew her.

Planes are still individuals—personalities—to the men who fly them in combat, and crews of the Eighth Air Force, to its very last days, named their planes and spoke of them in the possessive. It seemed to be a very natural tendency among otherwise normal, virile men to look upon the particular assemblage of machinery which they flew or maintained with some affection, to love it and pet it, and to think, usually, that it had certain characteristics which made it a little different from the others of its kind. Maintenance crews and combat crews had their own special plane for the first time when they reached the combat zone. Whereas in the training phases in the U.S. a crew never flew the same plane consecutively, except by coincidence, each combat crew had its own plane and ground crew. In the normal case that made a three way combination of loyalty unique in this world.

We had flown five missions before we got our own plane. We were as pleased as most crews when we were told one day late in June that our new plane was on the field. We flew it on a few practice hops and liked it. Everybody criticized his own department, and the summation of opinion was that it was a good ship. So far as pilots and engineer were concerned, the important thing was that it had four cool running engines and seemed to be economical on gasoline. It later proved to be an excellent ship from all standpoints. It was free of most of those many ills which can beset such a conglomeration of machinery.

The matter of a name had been bandied back and forth long before the plane appeared. Many a suggestion had come and gone but the ship was without a name and, therefore, devoid of personality when we flew it on its first mission. Several of our crew were married—including pilot, copilot, bombardier, and top turret—so we steered away from a personal name, to avoid partiality.

We flew the new ship on our sixth mission for her baptism of fire. The group bombed Sorau, and flak was intense. After an eternity on the bomb run, the ship gave that well-known surge, and bombs latticed out from all our formation. Navigator called and gave heading away from the target and ETA for the enemy coast. Then, after a pause, he added "Home, James!" That stuck. When we were on the ground again it was definitely settled that this was an appropriate name, all things considered.

Soon the inevitable female figure appeared on the ship's nose. The girl, a pretty young thing, held her skirt delicately with her left hand and thumbed a ride to the rear with her right. Over her head was the name "Home, James!"—if we may call it a name—and the heartfelt wish of us all. It should be added, in justice, that "Home, James!" never once came home ahead of schedule during her career and never failed to drop her bombs with the formation, even though, in another way, her name seemed prophetic.

As in the case of our ship, the names were not always feminine—if, indeed, they could be thought of as names in any sense. But planes were always referred to as *she* or *her*. And the woman usually came out in the picture, if not in the name. Every base had a few practical artists who could produce pretty faces and curvaceous figures on the noses of B-17s.

Our combat mess moved twice during our stay with the group. Finally, however, it was settled in a good location, and the mess hall was fixed up in an attractive manner. The mess officer, Major Ewald, hit upon a nice way of decorating the curving walls and ceiling of the long Nissen-type building. He employed a couple of soldier artists in painting the designs and names of all the planes of the base on them. The walls had been conveniently laid off in little rectangles of plywood in the original construction, so each name had its place. The job of painting was well done. At its conclusion, the mess hall furnished a very nice pictorial history of planes and crews that were or had been a part of the group.

So, even though our planes were numbers on the formation sheets, they were well-known personalities at their own home base. I remember some of these temperamental ladies of our group. "Baby Lou," "Salvo Sadie," "Queen Sally," and "The Careful Virgin" were among them. One ship pictured a beautiful creature reclining on a cloud bed in scant attire, and her name was "Heaven Can Wait."

Another had a sweet young thing in a bathing suit sitting on a block of ice. Her name was "Ice Kold Katy." Whether her name affected her fortune is hard to say, but the last time I saw "Ice Kold Katy," she was well on her way to elderly spinsterhood. Certainly, her name was appropriate to the subzero regions she frequented, even though her clothes were not.

Some of these ladies had reputations. Foremost among them was "Rosie's Sweat Box," upon whose nose was a pretty riveter, gun in hand, leaning wearily against a box and mopping her brow. It so happened that the pilot's name, Rozzell, had been shortened to "Rosie." His crew, therefore, hit upon this novel combination of his name, the feminine motif, and truth and reality for their ship. One would almost think, though, that they asked for trouble in calling their ship a "sweat box," for she turned out to be just that. She was the hard-luck ship of our squadron; so much so that crews disliked to fly her, on the few occasions when another crew other than her owners was assigned for a mission. She definitely attracted flak, and the miracle is that Rosie's original crew actually did finish a tour of missions intact. When the group returned from a tough mission, one could count on "Rosie's Sweat Box" being in the sub-depot for an engine change or for some first class skin surgery on her fuselage. Her original pilot, Rozzell, brought home a supercharger control box (it sits on a pedestal just between pilot and copilot) which had been shot away by a big piece of flak. The tail gunner of another crew was killed in the ship still later. I heard since returning to the States that this unlucky lady ended her career with a takeoff crash on an early-morning mission and killed all aboard.

As was suggested, "Home, James!" was another plane that took her name too literally. We flew eighteen missions in her, and she behaved beautifully. We always landed with an above-average amount of gasoline left, and we picked up comparatively little flak damage in all those eighteen missions. Sergeant Hirsch, our ground chief, had visions of reaching the twenty-five-mission mark without an abortion. At this point, he would have been entitled to an award for his good work. But it was pride in his job rather than the award that spurred him on. He and his assistants (Lawson and Jennings) went over her again and again before every mission, double checking everything that might force us to turn around and come home from a mission. Once, Miller (flight engineer) had saved them when an oxygen leak developed on our way over the Channel. Pressure started down in the system. We continued on our way while he made a thorough check of the lines. Fortunately, he found the leak and was able to repair it, so we continued the mission. Needless to say, we would have been forced to turn around had he not made the repair. We didn't go over Germany without oxygen—not even for our crew chiefs.

But between us all, we had a good record for the ship on the morning of her nineteenth and our twenty-sixth mission. This was when "Home, James!" decided to stay home for good. She sat in her dispersal area and caught fire on the preflight engine run-up, loaded with twenty-seven hundred gallons of gasoline and eight five-hundred-pound bombs. A fuel line on number three engine burst and sprayed high-octane gasoline over a good portion of wing and nacelle. In an instant, there was a dangerous fire going, there in the half light of early morning. Lawson and Jennings put that fire out with a portable fire extinguisher and their bare hands, while everyone else in the vicinity prudently ran for bomb shelters.

When the truck brought us out from the briefing rooms a few moments later, the fire was out, but our ship was ruined! We hurried off to a "ground spare"* and flew it on the mission.

For a while, we had hoped that the ship would be repaired. Finally, though, Mac (our engineering officer) told me that she was too badly damaged for profitable repair. She must be salvaged. We missed our ship, and we missed our ground crew more. For our remaining six missions, we were vagabonds, and we flew with various ladies of Mac's harem. I, for one, felt a definite twinge of sorrow every time I saw poor "Home, James!" sitting outside the big repair hangar. Like a beetle beside an anthill, she was being rapidly used up, for maintenance men can't resist spare parts.

Yet even this sad end had a consolation for us. Our ship had shown marked consideration for her crew in electing to burn on the ground rather than in the air. Had she burst that fuel line on takeoff, it is conceivable that Hirsch might have lost both ship and crew.

---

* Ship loaded with bombs and in readiness for the mission, in case of just such an emergency.

CHAPTER TEN

GROUND SUPPORT

10-1 Ground Crew-Repairing B-17 engines. Source: 401st Bomb Group Association

10-2 Chow line at Deenthorpe—Like the army, an air force travels on its stomach.

Source: 401st Bomb Group Association

10-3 614th Squadron Orderly Room—(L to R) Major Barr, base legal officer; Captain Mettlen, 614th squadron adjutant; First Sergeant Seiter; Sergeant Myers; Staff Sergeant Orgel.

Source: 401st BG Association Album (1948)

10-4 Maintenance shop-Deenthorpe Air Station, 401st Bomb Group.

Source: 401st Bomb Group Album, 1948

10-5 Medics—It is a sad testimony that when wars are fought, men will bleed and die. In this photograph, Major John H. Burke, 401st Group chaplain, has just administered final absolution as this airman is being carried to an ambulance.

Source: 401st Bomb Group Association Album, 1948

X. GROUND SUPPORT

The most striking difference between Air Corps combat units and most other such organizations was that air units consisted of two distinct echelons: ground and air. The proportion between these two echelons varied with the type of unit. In the fighter group, where the combat crew consisted of one man, the ground echelon by far outnumbered the air echelon; in the heavy bomber group, on the other hand, where a combat crew consisted of ten men, the total of personnel was divided about evenly between ground and air. The staff functions were divided between flying and nonflying personnel, with most functions occupied by flying personnel. On the group staff, for example, key positions were for the most part held by active combat flyers that were on operational status. The group commander, deputy commander, operation officer, group staff navigator and bombardier, and such assistants as they may have had, were rated officers. The group intelligence officer (S-2) and his assistants, the public relations officer, the group adjutant, the engineering officer (in some cases), the supply officer (S-4)), and other such administrative officers were nonflying officers.

In squadrons the division was about even. The squadron commander and operations officer were flying, and the adjutant and supply officers were nonflying. In all, headquarters there were a number of nonflying enlisted men who performed varied administrative functions. Aside from all these primarily administrative persons, there was the larger body of nonflying enlisted men in ordnance and maintenance work, photographic detachment, medical dispensary, flying control detachment, armament sections, and other such service functions. Corresponding to them—or rather, contrasted to them—was the great body of enlisted men and officers on the flying crews.

This basic feature—the clear segregation into flying and nonflying personnel—was the foundation for some interesting personal relationships, and also some interesting contrasts between air force and ground units generally.

The number of ground force troops who actually participated in combat as compared to those who served in rear areas was about in the same proportion as that between flying and nonflying personnel in the Air

Corps. The basic difference, however, was that the Air Corps setup was more clear-cut in this respect, and a man knew whether he was destined for combat or noncombat service in the Air Corps by the nature of his assignment. If he was in a nonflying job, he would not participate in combat, even though he may under certain circumstances have come very close to it. On the other hand, a man who went to the combat theater as a rated flying officer or enlisted man knew absolutely that, barring unwarranted circumstances, he would engage in combat repeatedly. There was none of the element of uncertainty or chance as to which category a man would fall into in air force organizations. By contrast, to consider infantry units, for an example, we might say that all personnel who were employed in headquarters from Division on up the scale, or who were in supply or service agencies in areas further back than a division headquarters were at best in a semi-combat status as compared to the men in the front line. A man could move into and out of a combat status from day to day, if the nature of his work took him back and forth between the actual combat area and rear areas of comparative safety. There could be no sharp dividing line drawn between a combat and a noncombat status in ground units such as was the case in all air combat organizations. No matter how far behind the lines, or how close to the front lines an air force combat unit happened to be situated, there were certain persons in that unit who were repeatedly in armed combat with the enemy and others who were not ever engaged in combat.

In the Eighth Air Force, a heavy bomber group was an ever-changing organization. The great body of the combat personnel was under continuous rotation, while the bulk of the ground personnel were more or less permanently assigned. Except for the key flying officers of the group and squadron staffs, who were required to fly their missions on a moderate scale, the flying crews came and flew their allotted missions or were shot down in action, generation after generation, while the same administrative officers and enlisted men carried on their duties in the group. The group was an administrative and operations framework through which passed the combat crews. Crews came and went while men who happened to be caught on the ground jobs stayed on.

Combat officers, first and second lieutenants by the hundreds, pouring into the long assembly line of bases between the training command and actual combat, often growled about the cloistered mess of permanent party officers, or the private club, as contrasted to the facilities for transients. It was certainly not uncommon to see PERMANENT PARTY ONLY signs on doorways to clubs or messes of the replacement depots and other installations that functioned primarily for the handling of transient crews. This was only reasonable, up to a certain extent, for the staff of permanent party officers on these bases was very small as compared to the great body of officers and men who were continuously funneled through them. It was impossible to provide all desired facilities for the transients but there was no reason why officers and men stationed at these places for an indefinite period should not make themselves as comfortable as possible.

This gripe, just like all others which ever arose in the services, had to be tied to specific cases. As far as I am concerned, there were certain establishments through which I passed that needed some reorientation as to the purpose for which those establishments existed. There were definitely some establishments where the permanent party attitude was about as smug and far removed from the real purpose of its existence, namely the serving of the transient personnel who passed through it, as could reasonably be conceived. Such places, of course, fostered by their attitude the very natural human instinct in men on their way to combat to be critical of the actions of all other establishments of that general nature. As a whole, however, it is certain that the job done in all these transient personnel bases far outweighed any justifiable criticism that would apply to a few of them.

There are good and bad features to all the jobs that must be done in our technical warfare of today (as of 1944). For the ground officers and men in combat groups, the indefinite—but in most cases, long—stay overseas was a bad feature. It was hard to see combat crews come and go and continue the same old job day in and day out. There was an intangible matter of morale involved. While they knew that all these jobs were essential, that they were necessary to the combat missions, it was hard for men of spirit to live constantly in the atmosphere of an intense existence and do prosaic and unexciting work daily. While the combat flyer's existence alternated between danger and relative security, between tenseness and relaxation, the ground men carried on with many routine jobs without the spur of nervous tension. When the combat flyer returned from a mission, he could mark up a definite and specific accomplishment and (what was more important, perhaps) he was one step nearer to completion of a tour of combat and a trip home on rotation. But the ground man went on day after day, and the end of the war was the only end he had in sight.

Discussion of this ground man-flyer relationship in the Air Corps is useful only in that it reminds us that a modern war requires every shade and variation of human effort and that if personal inclinations or desires were the guiding factors, we probably would not have even made a start toward winning the war. The same observation applies to any constructive building for peace. The Air Corps relationship was the perfect contrast between the two main classifications of service that go into the winning of modern war: the dangerous and wracking combat job, and the drudging and dull (but nonetheless important) job behind the battle. In each of these classifications, there were men who genuinely envied a man doing the other job, who gladly would have changed places and—in some cases, of course—could have done a better job by changing. It was the perfect setup for discontent, or for bitching and griping (as we say in graphic military parlance). It is good to know that, by and large, all the bitching was of a natural and healthy nature (which is inevitable), and that—though it was not always voiced—most of us had a lot of respect for the other man's job.

*   *   *

There were two authorities on combat planes, two kinds of knowledge. One was the knowledge of the maintenance man (as typified in the crew chief), and the other was the knowledge of the flyer (as typified in the pilot). Pilots and all other flying specialists were given maintenance training and had a general knowledge of the maintenance procedures for their equipment; and the maintenance men, likewise, had a speaking acquaintance with the operational procedures for the equipment that they maintained. A good pilot, for example, had a very sound knowledge of all the engineering features of his particular kind of plane; and a ground crew chief, by virtue of many test hops in his planes, was quite conversant with the flying of them, although he was not qualified to fly one himself. Despite the general familiarity of one specialist with the other's field, maintenance knowledge and operator's knowledge were two distinct fields, and an expert in one was a novice in the other.

There is no finer illustration of the complexity of modern combat planes than this fact: that it required one type of specialist or technician to maintain them and another type of specialist to fly them; and that within each classification of flyer and maintenance man, there was still more specialization. Although a good crew chief on a B-17, for example, knew his plane thoroughly and could have directed or performed any maintenance job within reason on any or all of its equipment, he had specialists to help him—ordnance men to fuse and load the bombs, armament men to check and maintain the .50-caliber machine guns (the combat gunners did most of the work on these guns), radio technicians to service and tune the three complex radio sets aboard, and instrument technicians to calibrate and adjust the many engine and flight instruments on the plane.

A good pilot, too, had a thorough knowledge of all equipment in his ship, as pertained to the operation of it. He was familiar with the operation of the gun turrets—each one a complex mechanism somewhat different from the others, the bomb sight and the allied bombing equipment, the radio sets, and the navigational equipment. But no pilot could hope to be master of all these things and there was no necessity for it. There were flying specialists on the crew for each piece of equipment, trained specifically for that equipment. The bombardier, navigator, radio operator, and the turret gunners were specialists for certain items of equipment and were proficient in handling of it. The aerial engineer, who was chief adviser and assistant to the pilot and copilot on all mechanical and engineering matters, and also manned one of the gun positions, was the air counterpart of the ground crew chief. Each of these several specialists performed certain functions which was necessary to the operation of the plane on a combat mission.

It may appear that this was laborious segregation of duties both on the ground and in the air. However, one combat mission would convince anyone that it could not be otherwise. In time, the members of a combat crew became familiar with the other's specialty, and to a certain extent, duties could be switched if and when it was necessary. This was even truer, perhaps, of the ground maintenance men—for often, they were forced to double up or consolidate their special jobs, particularly when the pace of missions was very fast. But on the whole, this division into the two main classifications of ground and air technician and into the more detailed specialties was the necessary rule.

*   *   *

The focal point of all this ground man-flyer relationship in a bomber group was the individual ground crew and combat crew on one airplane. There can never be any finer examples of cooperation and loyalty among men than were to be found here. We did not look upon it with any sentiment at the time, but in retrospect, we can know that never will Americans be privileged to live and work more inspiring relationships.

The ground crews did not number their hours or measure their effort in seeing that their planes were ready for missions. It was a matter of pride with the average ground crew that their plane would be ready for any mission for which it was called. During the spring and summer of 1944, ground crews literally lived in their planes during most of the hours when they were on the ground. In our own group, most crew chiefs lived in their line tents right next to the hardstands of their planes. They began work on their planes the moment they were landed from a mission and continued work all during the night and until takeoff time for the next mission in the early morning. During those days, the ground crews could portion their time for rest or sleep by the length of missions. While a nine-hour mission was certainly not a welcome prospect for a combat crew, ground crews could be excused for taking some satisfaction in them, for this was the only means for them to get nine hours of uninterrupted rest.

In the months of June and July of 1944, every available plane was usually called for on any day's mission. Combat groups had been stocked with planes and combat crews above the normal strength, and it was not uncommon for one tactical group to put up as many as three combat boxes (twelve ships each), or one airborne wing for a single mission. It had not always been possible to augment the maintenance personnel complements in proportion to this increase in number of planes, and the result was a terrific burden on the maintenance men. It has been pointed out that during the hectic days of those months, a scrubbed mission was not necessarily a blow to the morale of the combat crews. Men who were flying a schedule of three to five missions per week, ranging from five to eight hours, or longer, could reconcile themselves to having a mission called off, even if they had already gone a long way in preparation for it. But a scrubbed mission was no break to the maintenance men, for it usually meant that they would have to unload bombs—which would have been unloaded over the target had the mission gone off as planned—and that they would have to substitute for them a load of bombs of a different type. This changing of the bomb load was the worst feature of a scrubbed mission to all men who had anything to do with the readying of planes for missions. Often, however, the gasoline load had to be changed too. If a mission had been planned for a target in Northern France, planes would have been only partially loaded with gasoline, and it would be necessary to finish loading all tanks if the substitute mission, or the next mission, happened to be a deep penetration into Germany. So while combat crews may have wasted some effort on a scrubbed mission, they did not have to work nearly so much as the maintenance men did. While the combat crews could go back to the barracks and wait for the next call, the maintenance man began the wearisome job of first undoing what had been done, then starting all over again.

*   *   *

When a pilot and crew flew a plane other than their own, they were guests in someone's house. They were not only flying a plane that was normally used by some other crew, and which carried the stamp of their individuality as a combat crew in many significant little ways, but they were handling the property and the reputation of a strange crew chief. If possible, a plane belonged even more to its ground crew than to its combat crew, although it was always thought of in collective terms by both outfits. The crew chief's personality was always stamped on his plane. Freshly painted "butt cans" tied to the control pedestal and to other vantage points, extra relief tubes at strategic locations in the ship, a neatly lettered sign or notice to pilot or crew member here or there on the multitudinous gadgets, an extra slab of armor at one place or another, a reinforced windshield or an extra water container—these and many other items told something about the personality or the ingenuity of the crew chief. If you flew a ship that was immaculate and tidy in its interior arrangements, you felt duty bound to see that you did not leave it in an un-policed state. As a guest, you felt bound to conform to the rules of the house in as far as was possible.

I never flew a ship other than my own on a combat mission without receiving some tactful last-minute suggestions from the crew chief pertaining to what were actual or fancied special characteristics of his ship. Perhaps the flaps tended to creep a little; if so, he was sure to warn you about this and to suggest that the engineer could insert the hand crank and tie it in such a way that they could not creep. One of his engines tended to run a trifle hot, but there was nothing to worry about, and if you left the fuel mixture a little on the rich side, everything would be all right. Or perhaps one engine's oil pressure gauge registered a little below normal. It had been doing that for some time, and he just had not been able to get the instrument men out to fix it. These or any other particularities of his ship were invariably unknown to the strange pilot before he took off. While the crew chief's own pilot knew about these things and would not be disturbed by them, an alert crew chief wanted to be sure that a stranger did not needlessly abort his plane for some trifling mechanical reason if forewarning could prevent it.

While the crew chief was not a flyer, he was a rather shrewd judge of some pilot techniques, which were good or bad for a plane. If a pilot came wheeling into the hardstand at an excessive taxi speed and swung the ship around on a locked wheel, he was bound to take rubber off the pivot tire, and in most cases, that was like taking skin off the crew chief's nose. If he restrained himself from saying anything, his displeasure would be pretty evident on his clouded countenance. And when the pilot clambered down through the nose hatch, he was apt to find the chief fingering and examining the injured tire in mute reproach.

Ground crews habitually were on hand to see the crews return from missions. They grouped themselves near the end of the landing runway and watched the ships as they peeled off and landed. Certainly, their primary concern was the thrill of seeing their own ships and crews on the ground again. Even so, the crew chiefs could mix business with pleasure in this respect, and you may be sure that each noted the landing and taxiing of his own ship and that an unusually loud squeal of tires as his ship touched was a stab of pain to him, and that a smoking brake drum or a squealing brake did not go unnoticed.

No crew chief wanted or expected a pilot to continue on a mission if any mechanical trouble developed, which definitely made continuing a hazardous decision. Yet it is quite understandable that a crew chief felt very badly if his plane was brought back early without some very real ailment, or because of some trifling which made the abortion smack as much of timidity of the crew as mechanical trouble with the ship. Ground maintenance men were not showered with awards for their work, but there was a certain recognition and award due the ground crew of a plane that had completed a given number of missions without a mechanical abortion. In our group, the first such award came at the end of twenty-five missions. Therefore, it was a bitter disappointment to ground crews to see their ship land early.

I have seen a crew chief wait at the hardstand for his ship, which had returned early and was taxing around the field toward him. Knowing the suspense with which he waited, how disappointed he was and how he was wracking his brain to think what possibly could have been forgotten, I always felt that he was an equally pathetic figure as the chief who waited at the end of a mission for a ship and crew that did not come back.

An abortion from a mission was marked on the record as either a personnel or a mechanical abortion after an impartial examination of a ship after it returned. It was a personnel abortion if the pilot and crew returned needlessly or for some small matter which did not affect their safety; and it was a mechanical abortion if there actually was some mechanical failure in the ship, which made it necessary to return. The object was not primarily to lay blame on anyone, but merely to have a systematic means of laying responsibility where it belonged—for abortions were not to be tolerated beyond the inevitable minimum. When we speak idealistically of anything, we must qualify to allow for some failings of human nature. But it was a fine thing that the average pilot would spare no reasonable pains to keep from aborting a ship out of consideration for the crew chief, and that the crew chief, on the other hand, knew no limits for his labor spent in seeing that his ship was in perfect condition for the men who flew it.

When I think of the ground crews and their quiet, unsung loyalty, I inevitably remember that morning when our ship "Home James" decided to stay home once and for all.

Corporal Lawson was in the cockpit while Corporal Jennings stood on the ground with a fire extinguisher. Just as the number three prop was beginning to turn over, the engine gave a couple of deep coughs, and a sheet of flame enveloped the nacelle. In no time at all, the section of the wing near that engine was on fire, and the ship was a very dangerous place to be near to. Crews of other ships nearby saw the fire, and in a short time, that general area was deserted. A jeep sped across the field to the tower to summon the fire truck, and flares went up to tell the tower that something was happening on that corner of the field. In the meantime, those two men (Corporals Lawson and Jennings) stayed there and fought the fire with a portable fire extinguisher and their bare hands. The fire truck yowled across the field soon after the fire started, but it would have been entirely too late to stop a major catastrophe. Had Lawson and Jennings not put that fire out alone, the ship would have been too far gone by the time the truck reached it. It is quite possible that one corner of the field would have been blown up by those five-hundred pounders, once they got red hot in all that burning gasoline. As it was, the wing of the ship was warped and bulged by the fire, and there was one minor explosion in a feeder tank. No one ever found out how these two boys managed to stop such a fire with the equipment they had at hand, but we knew that they had risked their lives in no uncertain fashion and that they had averted a very serious catastrophe.

All I know is that when the truck brought us out from the briefing room, our ship was ruined and that a cluster of men were standing around, looking and marveling at the smoking wing and the bloated, warped nacelle of the number three engine. In the middle of the cluster—still grasping the empty fire extinguisher—was Corporal Jennings, and he was looking ruefully at the ship. What I will always remember is that he turned in a daze and said to Jack and me, "I tried to stop it, but I guess our ship's out for today!" That is what he said.

CHAPTER ELEVEN

THE LAST FIVE

Last Mission of "Chute the Works"
B-17, August 24, 1944

11-1 Last Mission: This photo was taken in the "debriefing" hut at Deenthorpe, England (August 24, 1944), following the last mission flying "Chute the Works" to and from Weimar, Germany. Crew members are from the 401st Bomb Group, 614th Squadron ("Lucky Devils"). Pilot, Captain J. F. Risher, Jr., on front row left. Copilot, Jack Refining; navigator, Lieutenant Harding; Bombardier, VE Brown, are on front row also. Eighth U.S. Army Air Force.

11-2 Comrades—Captain James F. Risher and B-17 crew comrades after surviving the thirty-second and final mission to Weimar, Germany (August 24, 1944).

11-3 401st Bomb Group B-17Gs in combat formation. These ships are from the 613th Squadron delivering a wake-up call over Lohne, Germany. The identifying marker for the 401st Group bombers was the diagonal yellow stripe on the vertical stabilizer (tail) as shown on these flying fortresses. The triangle S on the tail represents the First Air Division. Source: 401st Bomb Group Association

11-4 Visit to Deenthorpe (1993)—In October of 1993, my wife Joan Risher and I made a twenty-fifth anniversary trip to the United Kingdom. We made a side trip from London to Kettering, England, where we met with a local historian, Mr. Ron Sisney. He used to hang out at the Deenthorpe Air Station as a boy with the airmen of the 401st Bomb Group. He gave us a tour of the old base, including the beautiful marker donated by the 401st Bomb Group Association. Many of the old metal Quonset buildings are falling apart, but the old tower is still intact, and so was the runway. Farmers store hay in some of the old buildings. The roar of mighty Flying Fortress engines has been replaced by local model-airplane flying clubs, which use the old runway extensively. This was a wonderful short visit and made us even more appreciative of the tremendous sacrifice that all airmen, soldiers, navy, marine, coast guard, and merchant mariners made for their country in the world's deadliest war.

XI. THE LAST FIVE

As a combat crew reached a maximum efficiency in knowledge and experience, it lost its efficiency through physical strain and nervous exhaustion. This was the problem which faced the Air Corps in rotation of combat personnel: how to utilize experience to the fullest without unfairly and needlessly risking the crews beyond the limits of their physical capabilities, and without forcing them to continue combat missions beyond a reasonable chance of survival according to the indisputable loss percentage to which they were exposed. This was the problem that caused the Air Corps to set limits and restrictions on the rate of combat missions for key personnel or unit staffs. These men were subject to the same strain and the same mathematical chance of survival as all other combat airmen. In order to extend their experience over a maximum length of time, it was necessary for the Air Corps to retard their rate of missions. In so far as possible, this policy was carried out with all crews in lead positions. As the crews approached the end of their tour and acquired the maximum experience, they were deliberately held back from some missions and sent on others where their experience could be used to the best advantage.

The Eighth Air Force established the number of missions which constituted a tour of combat and which, when flown, entitled crews to a return to the United States and a new assignment. It was never the Air Corps policy that one tour of combat was a guarantee to a crew or an individual that no more combat flying would be required. The policy was to utilize a crew to its maximum capabilities, as established by medical study and the loss percentages on combat missions, and then to remove the crew from combat so that it might be used again to best advantage after proper rest, or that its experience could be used in the training of other crews. The primary consideration in establishing a number of missions for crews to fly was the availability of replacements and the needs of the Air Corps to carry out its mission. Within this limit—the number of crews on hand and available for replacement, and the number of crews required to accomplish the missions—the Air Corps regulated the number of missions for a tour on the rate of attrition or loss and, generally, on the character and intensity of enemy opposition, which was invariably reflected in the combat fatigue of airmen over a given length of time.

In the pioneer days of the Eighth Air Force—when enemy opposition was extremely fierce and when every small formation that went over enemy territory was under fighter attack—the loss rate was high, and twenty-five missions was a tour of combat. Considering the many trials of these early days, it is certainly probable that a man's chance of survival then was not as good as it was in 1944 and on to the end of the war, when the number of missions constituting a tour was raised first to thirty and, finally, to thirty-five. The latter figure was set sometime in June of 1944, and at that time, a formula was devised that gave crews credit toward the complete tour in accordance with the number of missions they had at the time. My crew had flown sixteen missions, and in accordance with this formula, we were credited with three additional toward the total of thirty-five and, thus, actually completed our tour by flying thirty-two missions.

So many factors contributed to the total of combat fatigue that it would be foolish (in my view) to attempt to say categorically which period in the history of the Eighth Air Force was the toughest on combat crews. After all, a crew or an individual who completed his tour at any time had reason to think himself very lucky, and those who were not so fortunate met a hard fate, which would have been the same at any time. In the early days the missions were shorter, less frequent, and for time in the air, far more rugged; in the latter days, missions were longer and more frequent, compounding the physical fatigue of one mission upon another. In all cases, the actual physical condition and the frame of mind that accompanied an individual through his last few missions depended most of all upon the kind of experience that he, as an individual and with his crew, had been through.

The unique aspect of combat flying over Germany in heavy bombers (and about combat flying in general) as compared to other forms of combat was that it was a clear-cut proposition. A man who embarked upon a tour of combat knew absolutely that he had a certain number of missions to accomplish; he knew the minimum number, even though he could not be sure that he might not be called upon to do more. There was none of the element of uncertainty or chance as to whether he would go through with this thing. It was a definite assignment that twenty-five or thirty or thirty-five times, he would take off with his crew in a loaded bomber and fly in formation over enemy territory and drop the bombs on targets which were, in all cases, defended actively—to a greater or lesser extent—by flak, or flak and fighters. For this specified number of times, at least, he would be over enemy territory for hours, where even a normal mechanical failure in his ship could be disastrous, and where most of the time that he was there, the enemy was opposing him, attempting vigorously to shoot him down. Though other forms of combat were harder according to all normal conceptions of physical hardship, there were few (if any) other forms which carried this specific psychological certainty of repeated conflict with an aggressive enemy.

Air, ground, and sea combat each had many ramifications. Men in tanks fought one kind of war, and they had their special problems and their special strains; airborne infantry had theirs; and the men who walked all the way into battle had their own. With the man on his feet, it must have varied somewhat depending upon whether he loaded and fired a big artillery piece, or moved behind a curtain of fire toward a point where his known enemy was waiting; and whether he fought in a stinking jungle, on a scorching desert, or among the hedgerows of a civilized land. In air warfare, a fighter pilot had problems and, no doubt, fatigue which did not apply to men flying bombers; and it was not even the same for pilots of night and day fighters. And the combat life of medium bomber crews was not the same as that of men on the heavy bombers. The navy combat crews of surface craft and undersea craft each had their special issues.

The general truth is that the various factors added up to the same final result. The variables were the intensity of effect and the time required for genuine combat fatigue to develop. Whatever the variables in special applications of these several types of combat, a general distinction can be drawn concerning the factors contributing to the total fatigue.

The ground soldier's fatigue was long drawn and continuous, compounded as much from the discomforts of his existence as from actual contact with the enemy. Actual physical suffering from the conditions under which he lived was very often the major part of his fatigue. As long as he was in the zone of combat, he remained in the atmosphere of battle. He not only sustained the risks, he moved in and through the wreckage. He buried his dead and his enemy's; he lived and fought in rubble and devastation.

Aside from the fact that medium bomber and fighter units often shared some of the ground soldier's living conditions of their own—in moving their bases rapidly forward—we may say that the flyer was free of these factors. For the most part, the flyer's fatigue stemmed directly from battle and from the strain of operating his plane or performing his proper function under battle conditions.

In the case of heavy bomber crews of the Eighth Air Force, an airman at his home base, snug in the English countryside, was as comfortable as a soldier could hope to be in wartime, and he was comparatively safe and away from the war. He could relax completely—sleep, eat, and play. He could lounge around his barracks and talk or go to town, see a movie. Or, if he sought another release, he could pedal a bike to some nearby English village, which remained as it was three hundred years ago. Here, his war would seem remote and very unreal. Physically, and to a lesser extent mentally, he was free of the war for a short time.

Then he went on a mission. For seven to ten hours, he was out in a never-never land of potential dangers and possible death. He was cold and uncomfortable and burdened with heavy equipment necessary to his existence in an alien atmosphere. He was imprisoned with his own crew in a steel and aluminum tube five or more miles above a hostile earth, surrounded by gadgets which could be his ruin or his salvation. Around him on all sides were oil, fuel, and oxygen lines which, if broken, could turn his metal tube into a torch. He was riding with several thousand gallons of high-octane gasoline and thousands of pounds of bombs—a lethal combination that did not always require enemy action to be his undoing. He was moving in and through a strange kind of "no-man's" land, where he could not live for three minutes without his oxygen mask and the slender tube which was his lifeline.

It was an existence of strong contrasts and strange unrealities. When a man left his warm bed in the early darkness for a mission, he was faced with three basic possibilities for the day: he would return to that bed and that barracks before night, he would be a prisoner of the enemy or a fugitive in hostile territory, or he would be dead. The result of this existence was a repeated stretching and relaxing of nervous fiber: extreme fatigue, then relaxation; tension and release. And all the while, the fiber was worn and lost its elasticity. It could be repeated many times, but gradually, the stretching had its effect. There was a limit where there was no stretch left, where the fiber remained taut and unrelaxed. The relaxation at the snug home base was not complete because it would not be lasting. Tomorrow or the next day, he knew he would go out again. Being at home was a respite, not a release. So many times he would do this, and only imprisonment or death or his own failure would intercede. It was a straight proposition.

Thus, men paid for the mental and emotional insulation that enabled them to live, act, and feel normally in a definitely abnormal way of life. Something of the normal feelings and reactions were sacrificed, at least temporarily, for it. It did not come for nothing. It was only afterward, months afterward, that one began to realize fully what must have taken place.

We might say that a normal tour of combat missions left a man with the world's worst hangover. This is, if we consider a hangover to be an abnormal condition of body and nerves brought about by repeated intense and unnatural stimulation. It was a prolonged hangover, resulting from repeated exposure to the intensifying effects of self-discipline and concentration on difficult tasks under extreme conditions of fatigue and danger. Some men found combat an irresistible drug. Its stimulation appealed to something in their nature, and they did not voluntarily relinquish it. The average man, however, was satisfied with the normal dosage required and was glad to return to a normal way of life to wear off its effects. But the hangover—the keyed-up nerve and the high-strung perspective—was present in varying degrees with all who touched the cup.

*   *   *

It was logical that when crews reached the stage of the last few missions, they dreaded the thought of missions more. Unconsciously, they began to feel that, since they had come through so many, they had literally used up most of their chances. As Harry Baker once said about us early in our tour, we were like young inquisitive puppies, and we were willing to try anything. At that time, we—like most crews—were anxious to rack up our score of missions, and we were not as battle-wise as we were to be in a few weeks. As we grew older in this game, we developed the philosophical attitude characteristic of seasoned crews. We were not greatly disturbed over scrubbed missions or over the many incidental things that irritated new crews. In the case of scrubbed missions, we simply shrugged our shoulders, so to speak, and decided that maybe this would not have been a good day for us anyway. But along with this seasoned philosophy, there developed also a deepening respect for each mission as a separate entirety and a specific step of achievement toward a long-sought goal.

As they gathered experience, crews came to look with a very practical eye on the relative toughness of different missions. According to any normal standard of living, there was no such thing as an easy combat mission. The very act of flying a heavily loaded bomber in close formation in varying and often trying weather conditions was in itself a radical departure from safe living, or even from normal flying activities here in the United States. Yet because of the heightened plane of existence on which we lived, a mission of a few hours over France or a short mission into Germany to a target thought to be lightly defended was actually looked upon as something easy, as the well-known phrase "milk run" would imply. Crews that went into the briefing room expecting a nine—or ten-hour grind into the heart of Germany felt only relief and satisfaction when they knew that they were going on a short one instead.

As a crew neared the finish mark in its tour of missions, these short and easy missions were appreciated even more. It is quite understandable that those who found that the target for the last or the next-to-last mission was Berlin or Munich or Oscherslaben did not feel that they had been blessed by chance or providence. There were some—of course, few in number—who could not take this as it came; there were some who deliberately turned around from a tough mission on the excuse of some mechanical trouble which was not evident when they landed. However, this number is so negligible by comparison with the great majority who went on, no matter what the target, that it is not fair to dwell on them.

I prefer to dwell on one particular pilot and crew whom I saw faced with a last mission and a very tough target. The pilot (Smith, we will call him, though this was not his name) had come through some fierce missions with his crew. Early in the history of the crew, they had aborted several times for rather flimsy reasons, and the abortions had gone on the record as *personnel* aborts. During the latter part of their tour, they had had a very excellent record and had flown as squadron lead on most of the latter missions. Then on the final morning, they found that Munich was the target. A long grind, lots of flak a certainty, excellent chance for fighters, deep over Germany, where it took hours to get back from the target to the enemy coast. Here, even one engine damaged or knocked out was a very serious business; no comparison between this and a short hop over France which, with better luck, they might have gotten. Only a week before, one of the veteran crews of the squadron, one which had about paralleled the history of this crew, had gone down on its next-to-the-last mission.

As I observed Smith in the squadron ready room after briefing and talked with him, I thought I saw a battle going on in his mind. Suppose he did abort deliberately from this mission. It would be marked up against him, and he would fly the next. There was a good chance that the next one might be easy by comparison. Then they would be finished. Whatever people might choose to think, it could never be *proved* that they had turned around out of cowardice, and anyway, they would be through. They would be going home. But if they went on this mission, there was certainly a stronger chance, according to all laws of common sense, that they would be shot down. Flak damage, which would not be serious over Northern France, could be their undoing several hundred miles inside Germany. It could be the difference between getting home safely and bailing out on the last mission. The last mission!

And then I saw Smith in the interrogation room after the mission. To say that he was excited, keyed up, drunk with the nervous reaction of being on the ground after grueling hours in the air would not distinguish him from any of us in the room. There is no feeling of satisfaction and relief, no sense of accomplishment to compare with the pent-up relief and sense of relaxation that came after a hard mission, no matter what the number was. But I believe that this pilot had an inward satisfaction, which would not wear off with the passing of hours. This was his last mission, but for other reasons also, this was an important day in his life. He had not turned back, he had continued; and he had added something to all his future by doing so.

When we went on missions into Northern and Central Germany, the formations skirted the Danish peninsula. Our path crossed the peninsula at a point where the enemy territory of Germany was a few miles to the right and the friendly land of neutral countries was a few miles to the left. Navigators tuned the radio compasses to the station at Malmo, Sweden, and as we made the turn into Germany, the needle slowly turned toward the tail of the formation. Sweden, of course, was the refuge of many stricken bombers on these missions into Northern Germany. And it was also a great temptation to any fainthearted crews among the formations. There was no force except the resolution and pride of the crews which could keep ships in the formation; if they chose to feign some trouble or take advantage of some relatively minor damage to their ships and go to Sweden rather than risk the long trip back over the North Sea, there was no one to stop them. It is certainly true that some crews wound up in Sweden which should have gotten back home, and would have if they had been more determined to get home. Probably some new crews went there without the slightest reasonable excuse. There entered the question of an indefinite period of internment in a friendly country as contrasted to going back to base to continue the tour of combat.

We do not intend to cast aspersions on crews which were interned in any of the neutral countries, or to suggest that any significant number of them were there out of anything but necessity. The tales of bombers coming home unbelievably damaged are too well-known to make this seem reasonable. Perhaps it adds to the credit of those who did drag home in crippled ships to know that they did so many times with a safe and sure refuge close at hand.

*   *   *

As we approached the end of our tour, it seemed to me that our missions had fallen naturally into three phases: the beginning stage, consisting of those seven flown prior to D-Day in the period from 7 May to 4 June; the long, hard middle stretch of missions, twenty in number, which were flown from 6 June to 24 July; and the last, excruciating five which began on 25 July with the mission to St. Lo and ended on 24 August with a mission to Weimar, Germany. We had time to savor the last drops of the experience at leisure during the month through which these five missions dragged.

In most respects, we had been an average crew. We had developed gradually from one lead position to another—first, element lead, then squadron lead, and finally, combat box deputy lead, which was our position on the last ten or twelve missions. It was in the natural order of things that our last few missions should be retarded, in accordance with the schedule of flying for lead crews.

After the terrific pace of missions in June and July, this deceleration in August arrested our motivation. The tour—which had flowed in a steady stream, leaving us sometimes too tired and stupefied at the end of the day to keep accurate tally of our missions from one day to another—now flowed to a trickle. And the last missions fell drop by drop, and painfully: 25 July, St. Lo; 4 August, Anklam; 13 August, Elbeuf; 16 August, Schkenditz (in Leipzig's cone of fire); and, at long last, 24 August, Weimar, Germany.

Actually, perhaps the days on the ground were more significant than the days in the air as we slowly finished our count. For the first time, it seemed, we had time to take mental stock of the situation while we were yet participating in this, the most unusual experience of our lives. There was to a certain extent an aching, apprehensive dread of the next mission, over and above what was experienced in the crowded days when missions piled one on top of the other. We felt heavy in experience and light in luck. This feeling characteristic of most men at this state of the tour, was accentuated by the fact that we now had ample time to entertain it. After our rather disturbing mission to St. Lo, when it seemed that we had used a large portion of our dwindling supply of luck, we had nine days while we waited for the next mission on 4 August; then nine more until 13 and 16 August; and seven between these and the final mission to Weimar. On the afternoons or evenings when I dropped in on the sergeants at their barracks or they came over to ours, they inevitably asked the question, "When are we going on the next mission?" They managed to sound nonchalant enough about it but I knew that they were suffering from the same kind of fidgets that I had, and that everyone else had at this time.

The mission on 16 August to Schkenditz was by actual count our thirty-first and next to last mission; but as a complete crew, it was our last—for Sergeants Ockerman and James Baker finished their count of thirty-two on that day, having gotten one ahead of the rest of us on substitute missions with other crews. We encountered some of the most accurate and intense flak of our entire career on this mission. Most ships in our formation—including our own—were damaged, and one ship was lost to flak over the target. This was one of those several occasions on which we actually smelled the cordite or powder smoke from the flak bursts.

As we turned on the bomb run, we saw that a sparse amount of barrage flak was popping over the target area at our general altitude, but it did not look very potent by comparison with some we had seen. However, as bomb bay doors opened and we settled down on the run, the characteristic three-burst blossoms of tracking flak began popping up ahead of the formation and in line with our flight, but several hundred feet too low. Quickly and surely, the line of bursts moved back to meet the formation, then moved ahead with it, and the number of bursts increased as more batteries joined the shooting. The bursts moved up and during the last thirty seconds of the bomb run they thumped into and around the formation, ahead of it and behind it, exactly on our altitude. And yet, even bomb runs—even the next to the last—must end sometime. The bombs floated away and we started the diving turn to the right. Even as these things happened, the ship gave the old familiar shudder, and Miller from his waist window, uttered an unintelligible exclamation over the interphone as a flaming burst, just outside his window, seemed to explode in his face. And, as a parting gesture full of venom, just when we heeled over in the turn to maintain our place in formation, a poisonous black, menacing, flower, larger than a cartwheel, blossomed instantaneously in front of our ship—so close that we saw its ruddy heart and breathed its heavy scent as it dissolved in smoke and passed through the ship.

The taste of flak was so fresh in our mouths when we landed that we felt that any more would have been an anticlimax. This should have ended it. Anyway, Ockerman and James Baker had finished, and the rest of us rejoiced with them. But it did not seem right that we would fly the next and last mission without them.

Very early in our crew acquaintance, it had become an accepted fact among us that Harry Baker was the most outspokenly religious man on the crew. Baker was a profound student of the Bible. I had discussed religious questions with him from time to time in our leisure moments in England and had been constantly amazed at his ability to back up his points with verbatim quotations, by verse and chapter, from various books of the Bible. Our religious discussions always left me in rather abject admiration of this man's knowledge of the greatest book of all. His religious convictions were not born in combat and would not end with the passing of danger. It was no reflection on the sincere faith of the rest of us that we all respected Baker for his more obvious and outspoken religious faith. In rather facetious token of this respect, we had long since declared among ourselves that we would not fly the last mission without Baker (Parson Baker, as already identified). We said that no matter who else might fly with other crews occasionally and thus finish early, Baker would have to stay along with the crew so that he could be on hand for the last one. And so he was.

*   *   *

Of the original ten, only six of us were aboard for the last mission on 24 August: Jack, VE, Jennings Miller, Mussetter, Harry Baker, and myself. Frank Ricks had, of course, not flown with us since early in our tour. Ockerman and James Baker had completed their tour—and declined to go with us, even for the sake of sentiment.* And Guy McClung, who had several more missions to accomplish, was replaced by Lieutenant Harding—a navigator who, like ourselves, had only one mission to go. S/Sgt. James Rhuman flew with us as tail gunner, and S/Sgt. William Berg replaced Ockerman as top turret gunner. Sergeant Croce, left waist gunner, had been removed from our crew a short time previously, in accordance with an Air Corps policy which eliminated that position from our combat crews.

Though Bob Ockerman and James Baker had finished, they thought enough about our last flight to get up at an unholy hour to see us off, and Croce was with them. They were down at the supply room as we gathered our equipment after briefing, and they rode out to the hardstand with us. They stood around looking a bit dislocated and lost as Sergeants Rhuman and Berg went about the business of preparing their old, familiar gun positions. While Berg was busy with the top turret, making those final adjustments which always partook of a man's individuality, Ockerman quietly entered the plane and placed the flak suits and helmets in the accustomed positions for Jack and me.

None could have been more conscientious and exacting than he had been in preparing his turret for all his missions. Thirty-two times he had painstakingly adjusted and tested it. But for all that effort, he had fired only a few short bursts at enemy fighters. We had been extremely lucky in this respect and had been in only a couple of brushes with fighters, though

---

* They would not have been allowed to go anyway.

we took the backseat for none in the amount of flak we had seen and encountered. Knowing how good these boys were with their turrets, how alert and ready they had been on all their missions, I had often privately thought what a shame it was that they had not had more chances to test and prove themselves. Thinking of this, I kidded Ockerman, just before we climbed aboard, that it was too bad he was going to miss all the fun today. I told him that our tour would not be complete without a good fighter attack and that he had just finished one day too soon to get in on the real fun. I thought I was kidding!

Once we were airborne, the last vestige of pre-mission nervousness, which had perhaps been accentuated today, fell away. This mission fell into a pattern like all the others, and it promised to be comparatively easy, though rather long—nine hours plus. Weather was good, with excellent visibility and only broken clouds at medium altitudes. The target, an aircraft factory near Weimar, was briefed as only moderately defended by flak. Formations were closely packed, and escorting P-51s shuttled back and forth overhead.

Harding had flown with us once before, and his voice and expression seemed familiar to me as he called periodically on interphone to give directions or navigational information. Rhuman and Berg had promptly and unobtrusively worked themselves into the customary interphone exchanges between gun positions, calling off observations on the formation and the fighter escort, checking for enemy aircraft as we crossed the enemy coast and drifted in over Germany.

Today, I noted and mentally fingered the many incidental details of the mission with a new interest. I put on and adjusted my oxygen mask as the altimeter needle wound beyond twelve thousand, and I breathed the familiar rubbery smell—the peculiar elusive blend of rubber and something else. It had become an accepted thing to my nostrils over long hours, and now I breathed it for the last time in combat with relish. I surprised myself by calculating that in the total of our missions, I had breathed that odor for the equivalent of at least one solid week. I noted how easily Jack and I changed control of the airplane, taking over and relinquishing the controls at a slight gesture or a glance; how each time the ship changed hands, she shifted position slightly in the formation, complying with the slightly different touch of two pilots. I allowed my eyes to travel according to long custom, and my mind noted how they moved: to engine instruments, noting each indicator hand in relation to the green; to oxygen indicators, where the little red balls moved up and down in their wells as we breathed; back to the engine instruments to check something that stuck out on the first glance; then a sweep down to the control pedestal where Jack's hand was lightly squeezing the throttles, easing them back and forth slowly as he flew; over to the radio jack box and up to the flight instruments (the altimeter, rate-of-climb, and artificial horizon); and then out to the formation—beyond it to the far edge of the sky, where possible danger lay, then down to the earth below.

I observed the formation and the escort, saw boxes and squadrons and individual ships in their constant, undulating movement, their continuous slight shifting of relative positions—ships within the squadrons, squadrons within boxes, and boxes within the combat wings. I saw the turrets wagging back and forth, up and down on adjacent ships; and the sun shimmering on spinning props, making them appear as transparent discs of glass. The planes themselves seemed almost motionless, hung by invisible rubber bands in this structure of planes, only bobbing slightly up and down, or moving gently to and fro.

And then came the thing which we had thus far escaped, but were not to escape entirely. "Bandits in the area," squawked VHF, and a tremor ran through the formations. I looked around and saw that our escort was nowhere to be seen; either the fighters had been tolled off by an alarm up ahead or behind, or we were being caught at the changing of the guard, when the old escort had been forced to go home and the new one had not arrived on the scene, through some mistiming. However it was, this time we were caught, for again VHF announced stridently, "Bandits at six o'clock!" I thanked Providence that on this day we had a wing leader who had always flown very close formation, continuously nudging the low squadron of our lead box into place, so that we in the low box sat now close under and just behind the lead box, within the protection of their turrets as well as our own. And in a passing glance I saw that such stragglers as there had been were shoving each other into place everywhere.

I took the controls and flipped my jack box to interphone in time to hear tail gunner call in a matter-of-fact tone, "Fighters coming up at six o'clock," and ball turret, "Wait till they're closer!" Jack and I exchanged quick glances of unbelief and then all turrets in the rear of the ship and the top turret above our heads opened fire. The ship shuddered and staggered with the blast. In my subconscious I heard bombardier in the nose announce plaintively, "Where are they? I can't see them." Neither could I. In the next ten minutes my formation fought a battle with twenty-five ME-109s, only one of which I saw for a fleeting instant. Three B-17s from our formation were shot down and, as determined by final tally hours later, all enemy fighters were shot down or damaged.

Our new tail gunner—who also was flying his last mission—turned out to be a cool hand and in the few minutes of our battle he and I worked out a system of cooperation which under favorable circumstances would have resulted in a lifelong friendship. He sat there in the tail, in the very muzzle blast of those ME-109s as they drove up behind us in tail attacks, firing until the last reasonable instant, then breaking away to swing tightly around and come again. He blasted with his twin fifties each time they came in range. And while he blasted, he judged the angle of their attack, watching the angle of the slim fuselages and the blinking of cannon in their noses. He called repeatedly, "Pull up a little. Pull up, pull up!" Or as they came around again in slightly different angle of attack—"Down, down, pull down!" Instinctively I followed his instructions, maintaining our place in formation, but easing back and forth on the control column, gaining and losing an allowable twenty feet of altitude. And up ahead of us, as the only visible sign of battle to us in the front of the ship, there appeared little ragged lines of gray puffs—20-mm cannon shells, bursting at their fused distance of four hundred yards. We moved down, and the ragged line burst above us; we moved slightly up again, and miraculously the gray puffs appeared below us.

Rhuman in the tail was not the only man in on this party, though he turned out to be the star performer. Berg in the top turret blasted each time the fighters came around, and he created a powerful stench of smoke in the cockpit. Mussetter was in the waist with Miller, each of them firing a waist gun. And Parson Baker raised hell in his ball turret. Out of the fragmentary babble on interphone, I heard him yell repeatedly, "I got him! I got him!"

The enemy fighters made approximately eight attacks on our formation, all from the tail. They flew almost directly in behind, firing as they came within range and continuing to the last reasonable breakaway point, sometimes within fifty yards. Each attack was marked by the crashing of the turrets and the ragged line of 20-mm puffs in front. At each breakaway the turrets silenced, the gray puffs disappeared, and the interphone became alive again with excited fragmentary snatches of words:

"There goes a B-17."
"Look at those babies turn!"
"Boy, I got that one, sure!"
"There go the parachutes."
"Here they come again!"

This last announced the end of every break. A pause, and the turrets staggered the ship again in the irregular bursts of fire, and the gray puffs appeared like evil genii in front of us, above, or below us as we moved slightly up or down.

I looked out my window at the end of a pass in time to see a bomber of our low squadron rear like a stricken horse and plunge over on its back in a last long dive. And then I saw the fighter which probably had fired the fatal bursts swing up and out, pausing at the height of his climb and diving to our rear for another run.

At last, there were two fighters left and a crippled B-17 behind our formation. I heard on interphone, "They're going after that cripple!" And then, seconds later, "Zoowie, she got 'em both—and she's still flying!"

And that, quick and easy as it seemed, was our last real contact with an enemy in the air. For us, and for crews in all the other ships which continued in formation to the target and dropped our bombs, the whole episode had been only a quarter hour. The intensity of those few minutes was evident not in what had transpired or what we felt or saw at the time, but in later reaction. The rest of the mission seemed insignificant by comparison. As we continued, leaving the unmarked, empty space of the battleground, it seemed absurdly impossible that men had just died there; that some who attended briefing with us four hours ago had abruptly stopped thinking and feeling and seeing forever, just in the last few minutes. Riding on four engines in a lightly damaged plane, it was strange to know that other crews were now in the ordeal of the long trip back home in crippled planes—some to lose the struggle in bailout and capture, others to end it hours hence in crash landings somewhere in England.

*   *   *

Ockerman, Baker, Croce, Frank Ricks, and "Mac" were at the hardstand when we taxied in. It was good to see them there and to know that they had shared with us, as much as they could, this last flight. It was good to see Hirsch, Lawson and Jennings, our old ground crew, who still regarded us as their crew, despite our bad luck with "Home, James." Ockerman and Baker could not conceal their disappointment when they heard what had happened on the mission. Obviously they were sorry they had missed the battle; and we were sorry also, though we were now fast friends and comrades of the three strangers who had flown with us today.*

When we were gathering the guns and equipment at the end, I suddenly realized that never again would the ten of us board the same airplane at once. There would be no more practice missions for us and no more combat missions. This was indeed the last mission.

My mind flashed back over a few crowded months and I seemed to be looking down a vista of years.

This was late summer. Could it be possible that only this spring we landed our new B-17 on the little field at Nutt's Corner, Ireland; that we were hustled out with all our baggage into that toy land of tiny green fields and doll houses, and the plane departed before we had time to collect our thoughts? Was it this spring, last year, or last century that we made the long journey by water and rail from Ireland to Scotland and then down through England to Stone, to Bovington and thence to this base? How long ago was it that we rolled on the Irish Sea, slept on our straw pallets in Lorne, and played hearts all the way to England on the train, even while filled with the heady excitement of being in a strange land on an unusual sort of journey? Then a pub was a novelty, traffic in pounds and shillings a new satisfaction, and ancient England was a land of new discovery.

---

*   By final assessment of all conflicting claims of gunners in the formation, our gunners received confirmed credit for three ME-109s: one to tail gunner, one to waist, and one to ball turret. Top turret received credit for a damaged.

An assortment of recollections, trivial in themselves, flowed by and blended into the pattern of our total experience.

Mussetter and Brown and their two bottles of Irish whiskey, purchased in Belfast. Mussetter had dropped one as he boarded the train at Lorne. A wail had gone up from the long waiting line as the smell of good whiskey floated up and out. Brown had found the other bottle crushed in his handbag when he pulled it out of the baggage car, and had thrown the whole reeking bag away.

The days of waiting at Stone and Bovington when we went to school again; the waiting and wondering where we were going next, so reminiscent of the whole training cycle. The first air raid alarms at Bovington, and the sound of enemy planes overhead in the dead of night. The first sight of formations going out for missions in the morning and returning in the late afternoons, and the knowledge that we would soon be among them.

The first days with our group. The thrill of completing the first mission, and the first five; the growing confidence as the total of missions steadily mounted—the unspoken satisfaction at the end of each one that at least we had come this far.

Practice missions on our off-operations days, sometimes fun and sometimes boring. Occasional ferry trips, when we took uninhibited jaunts at low altitudes to other bases, picking up or delivering a plane. Afternoons on the skeet range, when Mussetter or Harry Baker invariably collected the pot of half a pound each. Bail out and ditching drills, when we practiced what we hoped we would never have to do.

Quiet dull days in barracks, under cold and soggy skies, when we fought the gnawing restlessness; crowded, harrowing days in the air when we flew from dawn to dusk, and Death so often kissed us and passed us by.

Certainly we had come to the end of a singular and, memorable event in life. So many things had happened in such a short space of time. Neighbors of thirty years acquaintance in a normal life could hardly have so many vivid recollections of common experience as we ten who had been total strangers less than a year ago. Even now we knew comparatively little of each of the other's background; strange that in wartime associations these things are often passed over. And yet I knew each of these men better than I knew my closest relatives or my dearest friends in civilian life. From Arizona, California, Ohio, New York, South Carolina, Iowa, Texas, Minnesota, and Massachusetts—we had by chance been banded together. We had come to think that any other combination would have been wrong, even while we knew that thousands of combinations as diverse had worked as well.

The end of this mission was for us one of those experiences of a lifetime, which can be felt but never adequately expressed. Relief and joy at the completion of a great duty—the greatest in our lives to date—was strangely blended with a vague regret.

CHAPTER TWELVE

AFTERMATH

12-1 Victory—Catholic Service at Deenthorpe Air Station on VE Day
(Victory in Europe).

Source: 401st Bomb Group Association

12-2 Care Packages—A B-17G dropping boxes of food instead of bombs for civilian refugees in Holland (1 May 1945). The War in Europe ended 7 May 1945.

Source: United States National Archives photo

12-3 The Scrap Yard—The final resting place for surviving WWII bombers, to be scrapped and recycled for more peaceful uses.

Source: North Star Galleries

12-4 Converted—A U.S. coast guard PB-1G Air-Sea Rescue B-17. A rescue boat is mounted beneath the fuselage, from where bombs once dropped. A chin-mounted radar dome replaces the forward machine-gun turret of wartime bombers.

Source: U.S. Coast Guard photo

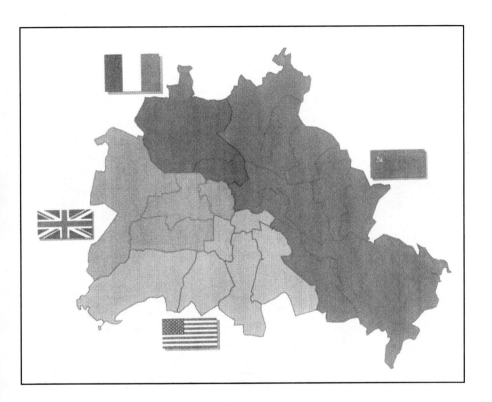

12-5—Postwar Division—The map shows the occupation of East Germany by the Soviet Union, and West Germany governed within zones occupied by the United States, Great Britain, and France.

Source: Wikipedia Encyclopedia

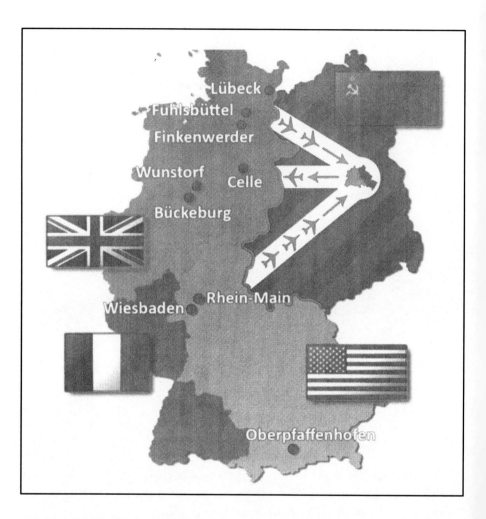

12-6 Berlin Blockade—The map shows the occupation zones of the United States, Great Britain, and France, and the general air corridors for cargo flights by military transport planes to Tempelhof Airport, Berlin (1948).

Source: Wikipedia Encyclopedia

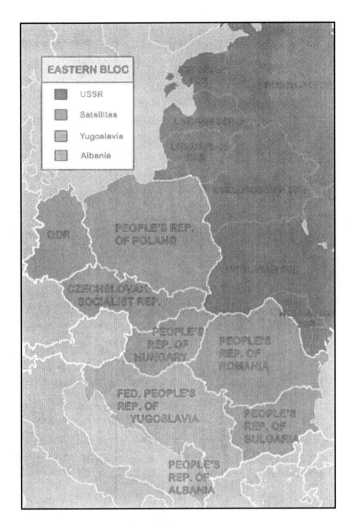

12-7 The Eastern Bloc—Map shows the post—WWII domination of Eastern European nations by the Union of Soviet Socialists Republics (USSR). WWII brought Poland, Czechoslovakia, Hungary, Romania, Bulgaria, and East Germany (German Democratic Republic) under Soviet Communist Control.

Source of map: Wikipedia Encyclopedia

12-8 Tempelhof—U.S. Air Force and Navy Douglas C-47s (Navy R4D) unload at Tempelhof Airport during the Berlin Airlift.

Source: U.S. Navy National Museum of Naval Aviation

12-9 Berliners—Children of Berlin stand on a pile of war-damaged rubble to watch a Douglas C-54 Skymaster approach for landing at Berlin Tempelhof Airport in 1948. The approach to Tempelhof was dangerous. Pilots had to fly between tall apartment buildings and then make a steep descent to the runway, often flying on instruments in foul weather.

Source: United States Air Force photo

12-10 Hero of the Airlift—Air Force Lt. Gail Halvorsen, the "Candy Bomber." He personally created immense goodwill with the people of Berlin, especially children, by dropping bundles of candy attached to small parachutes made from handkerchiefs, as his C-54 would approach the Tempelhof runway. Lieutenant Halvorsen's candy parachutes soon caught on, and other pilots followed his example. His fame was noticed and supported by the hard-driving commander of Airlift Operations, General William Tunner, and even President Truman. Gail Halvorsen was pronounced a hero back in the States.

Source: U.S. Air Force photo

12-11 Spy Fortress—An RB-17 reconnaissance aircraft of the U.S. Air Force 7499th Composite Squadron based at Furstenfeldbruck Air Base, Germany. This wartime bird had armaments replaced with cameras and electronic eavesdropping equipment for intelligence-collecting operations on Soviet military forces and installations. The RB-17s roamed the skies from the Adriatic to the Baltic Sea, monitoring Soviet activities during the "Cold War." They also jammed Soviet radar during the Berlin Airlift. The 7499th used other aircraft also, such as the C-47 and B-26 Invader, and later C-54s. The photograph was taken about 1950.

Source: U.S. Air Force photo

12-12 Former enemies, new friends—A Thirty-Sixth Fighter Wing—sponsored sports competition event for German youths from Furstenfeldbruck, Bavaria (1949). The Thirty-Sixth was the first U.S. jet fighter wing sent to Europe in July 1948 in response to the Soviet blockade of Berlin. U.S. Military—and Red Cross—sponsored activities helped foster understanding and trust between U.S. soldiers and former enemies during the postwar occupation. The two pictures show German citizens in traditional Bavarian dress, and a U.S. Air Force staff sergeant (far right). Major Jim Risher (Thirty-Sixth Fighter Wing) and Betty Risher are shown (far left) presenting competition awards to young Germans. Note the soccer field and goal in the background located on the former German Luftwaffe air base.

Source: Thirty-Sixth Fighter Wing, U.S. Air Force photograph

XII. THE AFTERMATH

The Second World War (1939-1945) was the most destructive and widespread conflict in human history. By some accounts, fifty million to seventy million people perished—military and civilians. WWII was fought on nearly every continent and ocean. More than one hundred million military personnel were mobilized for combat worldwide. The War's participants organized entire economic, industrial, educational, and scientific systems and civilian workforces into the support of military forces. The mobilization of entire societies to support war made the targets of destruction by Allied and Axis opposing forces indistinguishable between military and civilians. More than any previous military conflict, World War II was marked by millions of civilian casualties and, uprooted and displaced refugee populations of all descriptions, and within all the theaters of combat.

The most horrific assault on civilian populations was the targeted, intentional destruction of ethnic and religious populations, as an element of national policy. Upon the ascension of Adolph Hitler and the Nazi Party to rule Germany in 1933, he and his fanatical followers and henchmen directed a national policy and programs—through state-run propaganda and other means—to discredit and disenfranchise Jewish people, ethnic minorities, and developmentally disabled people, blaming them for Germany's social and economic ills following its defeat in World War I (1914-1918). An ominous, propaganda-orchestrated process of intimidation, seizure of property and businesses, and removal of citizenship rights escalated to the displacement, enslavement, and mass murder of millions of people—not only in Nazi Germany, but in its other conquered territories as well. The Holocaust was stopped only by the unconditional surrender of Nazi Germany and its allies to the Allied Forces on May 7, 1945.

Japan followed a similar pattern of cruel oppression of civilian populations in the Pacific before and after its sudden attack on the United States by aircraft carrier—launched planes on December 7, 1941, at Pearl Harbor, Hawaii. The Japanese militarists enforced its control of conquered territories in Manchuria, China, Korea, and the Philippines by murdering hundreds of thousands of civilians, by every means possible. World War II ended in the Pacific on August 15, 1945, after the United States dropped two atomic bombs on Japan, causing thousands of civilian and military deaths in Hiroshima and Nagasaki. The first use of atomic weapons was weighed against the certainty of hundreds of thousands of American casualties that would have occurred through an invasion of the Japanese Islands. The Soviet Union was one of the Allies in WWII—but the Communist regime of the dictator Josef Stalin brutalized their own people to enforce the policies of the Communist state.

World War II's end did not end conflict—it fostered new world conflicts. While the former Allied Nations moved toward occupation of their defeated enemies and rebuilding them, the Soviet Communist regime, led by the brutal dictator Josef Stalin, flexed its expansionist aims for ideological and territorial expansion. What had been one Germany had become East and West Germany—and Berlin's occupational rule was divided into a Soviet sector and American, British, and French sectors. The sudden onset of the Soviet Union's blockade of Berlin in June 1948 clearly marked the beginning of what we know as the "Cold War"—lasting four decades, ending only with the economic collapse of the Soviet Communist system.

The United States and its Allies' Berlin Airlift operations spared the people of Berlin from starvation at the hands of the Soviets. The airlift forced the Soviet armies to back down and lift the blockade on May 12, 1949. The Berlin Airlift was ended October 1949 and was one of the greatest humanitarian rescues of all time.

*   *   *

Following his Eighth Air Force combat tour, our father returned home to rejoin his wife and our mother, Betty Risher, at the Boca Raton army airfield in Florida on October 1944 as a radar pilot instructor with the 3501st USAAF Bomb Group. Ironically, after thirty-two aerial combat missions, he was involved in a runway accident on a training mission in a B-24 when it collided with a B-17 on February 5, 1945. Both aircraft were destroyed in the collision, but all crewmen escaped the crash, thanks to air base firemen and local volunteer firefighters. Father had a finger on his hand amputated when it was mashed into the instrument panel from the impact, as he was in the copilot seat. After assignments at the Army Command and Staff School and a Pentagon assignment as assistant editor of the history of the Ninth Air Force, he returned to the 3501st, and the Air University System at Tyndall Airfield, Florida (I was born by this time—July 22, 1946).

Our family joined up with the Thirty-Sixth Fighter Wing at Howard Air Force Base, Panama, in March 1948 (by this time, the Air Force had become a separate service—by order of President Truman). Father was the personnel officer in the Wing's Headquarters Squadron. The Soviets began the Berlin Blockade, as previously mentioned, in June 1948. In July 1948, the Thirty-Sixth Fighter Wing was sent to Furstenfeldbruck, Germany. It was the first jet-fighter outfit in Europe, with new Lockheed F-80 Shooting Stars. Furstenfeldbruck was a former Luftwaffe airfield. Major Risher helped organize the Wing's move and find housing for airmen and their families. (My mother and I were among the first family dependents in occupied Germany).

Major Risher, like many multiengine-rated pilots, was pulled into flying cargo missions to Berlin, flying the Douglas C-47 Skytrain and Douglas C-54 Skymaster. In October 1949, he was appointed as executive officer of the 7499th Composite Squadron, which was a top secret outfit, flying photographic and electronic reconnaissance missions to gather information on Soviet military forces.

This summarizes the background for the post—World War II experience. Our father's writings presented herein focus on two aspects of his postwar observations. The first is an afternoon visit to Dachau, the longest-serving Nazi slave-labor camp during Adolph Hitler's regime. Unfortunately, there are some pages missing from his narrative about Dachau, so we have tried to piece together what we have from the previously mentioned file "Major J. F. Risher—miscellaneous correspondence and writings." The Nuremberg trials of Nazi war criminals were also going on at this time. The Dachau narrative recalls back to the story he learned as a child, about the death of Ed Haley at the old country church near his farm community. This may be somewhat repetitious, but is relevant to the observation about mass death and enslavement at the horror place, Dachau. As presented in the narrative, we learn by contrasts. The second narrative concerns the return of veterans and the propensity of our nation to disarm too quickly in the face of new threats. This narrative rings true today. We have only to recall the horrible attack by fanatics on our country on September 11, 2001, to remember that freedom requires preparation and constant vigilance.

James F. Risher III

ROAD TO DACHAU

This afternoon I took the road to Dachau. I had been in this neighborhood, based at Furstenfeldbruck, some time before I realized that I was so near this famous and infamous spot. Perhaps you remember the place from your reading of the news? In case you've forgotten, Dachau is that one of several famous German concentration camps. It accounted, in various ways, for the lives of some 238,000 persons of all European nationalities during the several years of the Nazi regime. This particular camp is located on the outskirts of the town of Dachau, in that most beautiful and pastoral part of Germany known as Bavaria.

It so happens that this place is only 18.5 km from our air force base at Furstenfeldbruck, and so this afternoon I was able to step out of our Wing Headquarters building and drive a few miles through a most beautiful rural countryside out to the edge of the Dark Ages.

We cannot really experience except by contrast. I'm glad that I saw this place on a quiet autumn afternoon, after a ride through the most peaceful rural scenery imaginable. At one time this camp was a horror spot. Now it is only a nondescript arrangement of stone and frame buildings, preserved by our occupation forces for whatever meaning they may have to those who would come and stand on the spot.

Imagination is quickly palled at contemplation of such a place as this. You know the facts—over two hundred thousand persons enslaved and exterminated here by all conceivable means of starvation and torture; human bodies stacked and burned in these furnaces, now standing naked and clean on their concrete floors. The people brought to and enslaved in this place by the Nazis lost everything (families, friends, and livelihood) and the most important direction to human destiny: the power to choose.

I turned homeward on the winding road from Dachau, moving slowly past scenes of thrifty rural plenty. I passed heavy wagons, pulled by slow moving oxen, loaded with turnips and hay and topped by healthy, ruddy faces; passed well tilled fields where men, women, and children were at work, breaking ground or gathering the fall crops. I passed through the small, stone, thatched villages—Eisnach, Esling, Maisach—breathing the earthy animal smells of the barnyard, stopping for slow-moving herds of cattle in the road, seeing the stir of evening activity in barns and farmhouses. Life—bustling, purposeful. Yet I thought of Death, remembered again my first awe of it, and realized that what I had seen at Dachau was, in my own experience, the third concept. My mind went back again to the first concept.

*   *   *

When I was a boy, there was one spot in the countryside around my home which was strangely marked. Near my home was a little country church, long deserted. Once, years before my time, it had been the place of worship and the community rendezvous and gathering spot for most of the people who lived in that section. They came and sat on the hard, straight benches and listened to the long sonorous sermons of many a fire-baiting preacher. They stood around under the trees after the services and talked—the women in a cluster by the front steps, the men gathered to one side under a giant oak. The air was filled with the sound of slow, unhurried voices and the smell of tobacco from strong pipes. And then, one by one, the family groups collected, and wagons and buggies moved out from the grove of trees and went their separate ways. This went on for years. Life was unhurried among these people, and unspectacular.

But even here, the collision of separate human destinies and desires could be tragic, and was. One Sunday morning after church, the congregation stood around as usual and talked in leisurely fashion. But two men stood off to one side under a small oak and talked—at first in quiet tones, and then heatedly. One pistol shot rang out, and the drifting tobacco smoke took on a pungent smell. John Edwards had killed Ed Haley there under the little oak, and this place was forever changed.

The killing was many years old when I first knew of it, but the place was marked in memory. The church, long since deserted, stood as a forlorn and ghostly skeleton, half hidden in the tall grove. The colored folk avoided the spot, and it was seldom that anyone had occasion to go near it. It stood—and still stands—in that community as a symbol of the tragedy of unnatural, violent death.

There in England, on occasional summer afternoons when some of us who were not flying the mission lay in the sun outside our barracks and dozed or talked, I thought of my first and only visit to that little church. I remembered how strangely fascinated I was by the thoughts that arose when I stood under the tree, which marked the spot of this old tragedy. "He fell right under that oak," my uncle had said as we walked through the old churchyard on the way to one of his fields, "and he was dead before they picked him up." He had pointed to a sizeable tree standing some ten yards or so from the crumbling walls of the old building. This tree had been a mere scrub twenty years ago when Ed Haley died under it. Twenty long, slow, monotonous years had slid by this place since a man had died prematurely here. The tree had grown, the building had crumbled, the witnesses of the tragedy had long since scattered. And yet, had he not died violently, because of some entwining of human destinies unknown to me and forgotten now by most of those who knew, he would have been a middle-aged man: a robust, hearty, plain-living man typical of this part of the country.

Twenty winters and twenty summers had passed this place. Breezes had rustled the leaves of the tree in the summer, year after year, and winds that rattled its branches in winter; and all the long years it had grown, slowly but inevitably, while a man who should have been alive today, and in his prime, had long since dissolved into nothing. He had died obscurely, but his death had been marked as far as his life would have reached. This spot, this very spot, was the place where—in a single moment of violence—one life had been ended, and others had been forever altered and transposed within their spheres. Whether the man had died by his own misguided actions or those of his killer, whether or not his killing had been justified by the laws of the land, was now of no consequence. A fundamental fact of human existence, the final and irrevocable fact, had been enacted here.

*　　*　　*

Then I was in England, at my wartime bomber base. Here I learned the second concept. I had been forced to contemplate Death as a part of the strange existence I led.

The natural impulse to fear and revolt against known danger, was constantly pushed into the background. And this was the second concept, for though we had not lost entirely our fear of Death, we had become acclimated to an unnatural existence where normal fears and reactions were suppressed. We had been forced into an unseasonable familiarity and to a great extent had actually developed a certain callousness and contempt. Contemplation of Death had lost the tragic and beautiful overtones. Here it was a casual, commonplace thing, no matter how regrettable. We could believe—we had to believe—that Death had a purpose here. But we knew that this exposure had been superimposed upon normal existence, and to that extent, we who were exposed had lost our identity and individual purpose in life.

Here in England, I could not think of Death as intensely as I had on that first and only visit to the little church. For in this English countryside, peaceful though it was, we were living on a plane which did not encourage or allow us to think in that way. For the time being, at least, it must be viewed coldly and logically. It was simply a rate of attrition in an unusual sort of enterprise. For the time being, an exploding bomber could not and would not be thought of as the tragic death of ten young men, their hopes and potentials lost forever, but as part of an inevitable loss percentage. Though a tractor ticked away on a distant hillside and the air was filled with the universally peaceful smells of the country, empty bunks must be thought of as available bunks and personal effects of the men shot down, as military baggage for shipment. The change in thinking had not been forced; it had been inevitable.

*   *   *

Now here was Dachau and the third concept of mass and ignominious death. This afternoon, I had seen the place where the individualism of humanity had been liquidated; where Death, a fundamental experience of living, had been foully cheapened and relegated to the status of a stupid, commonplace happening of absolutely no consequence. Death here did not pluck at the entwined strings of human destinies, for it obliterated whole families and communities; it did not inspire, for it was too commonplace; it did not frighten, for there were more things to fear in living. This to me is the real meaning of Dachau. True, we must remember this place as a symbol of the brutality of which the German people were capable under Nazi rule and must require them to redeem themselves before the world; but Dachau is, even more, a symbol of that threat to man's dignity which still hovers over the world. The facts of enslavement, torture, and horror here are significant and terrible to contemplate; but the real horror is in the thought that mankind all over the world might yet conceivably be subjected to mass death—as purposeless and meaningless to the individual and as contrary to human development and advancement as the destruction of families, deaths, suffering, and enslavement of Dachau's two hundred thousand.

There *is* this threat to the world. We must realize now that mankind has it in his power to create a hundred Dachaus overnight. No torture, perhaps, no inhuman suffering, no lingering deaths—just wholesale extermination. Just the sudden vaporization of thousands of human bodies in a flash—a mass cancellation of hopes and fears, abilities and aspirations, beliefs and ideals, plans and potentialities.

I am, in a way, a technician of this wholesale extermination. And perhaps you are too, or will be. You and I would not torture or starve our fellow man, and we earnestly believe that an institution such as Dachau could not exist within our borders. But let the die be cast, and you and I will be parties to mass slaughter. Without malice, purely in a technical or professional way, we will push a button or fly a plane or draw up a plan of operations or machine or instrument of destruction. We will expedite production, allocate manpower, formulate long-range plans. We will scan radar scopes, calibrate and read delicate instruments, tune and direct ultra-frequency radio waves. We will take from the ground certain materials we need, or make them artificially. We will—in a thousand and one ways—divert and channelize our boundless energies and abilities to the end destruction of humans on a colossal scale.

We do not want to do this. We do not even want to return to concept number two, where we are forced to look unnaturally upon the fundamentals of living, think and act in a way that is forced by a slow conditioning process, for this is the twilight zone between the two extremes of light and darkness. We would rather let the world regain its health and its sanity, let displaced persons find for themselves a home and a life, let all the present wreckage be removed and replaced by the indefatigable energies of man. We would rather return to concept number one and look upon the death of individual man once more with awe and reverence, mark the place, remember the circumstances, consider the implications.

VETERANS*

If America is to be a land of lobbying, pushing, pressure groups in all the years ahead, a land whose citizenry are too intent upon advancing selfish interests within our own structure to cast an eye or a thought to the world outside, our years will be numbered and we will be utterly unworthy of such time as is allotted us to exist. If any people were granted time and opportunity to gird themselves during the struggle for the duties which must come after, the American people were granted it. We are the only major power engaged in this war which was not forced to undergo all the trials of the struggle as a people. We are the only nation which was not actually invaded and pounded by the forces of an enemy in one way or another. And yet the same old themes grip us: down with the army, down with controls and restrictions, up with my wages, let the rest of the world look out for itself.

When we say that the average citizen today is grossly selfish and narrow in his thinking, we mean just that. There *is* a line and a distinction that can be drawn between selfishness and unselfishness in outlook, and the majority of American citizens must discover it or rediscover it if we are to be worthy of our place in the world. It is not sufficient that we, individually and collectively, are lovers of liberty and the good things of life, and that we have been willing to fight for them when we were forced to it. How can we fancy ourselves unique in this respect? And yet, considering our reactions to the problems arising with the end of the war, what else can we say for ourselves? We can say, certainly, that we have never forced aggression upon another nation and that, powerful as we are, there is no nation on the face of the earth which need have any fear of us. We know that this is true and it is a fine thing for us to know. We can have great pride in this fact. It is a fine thing to know that this nation, which at the moment is one of the two most powerful on the earth, and which now holds the most terrible secret of destruction known to man, has absolutely no designs for conquest or aggression. It is bracing to our faith in human nature that, despite all our unworthy internal struggles, this is certainly true.

But this is a negative attitude and it is not appreciably more than the smallest and weakest nation in the world can say. Our place irrevocably

---

*   written August, 1948

demands that we go further. It demands that we face the world with force and overwhelming influence for peace and order among nations.

The time has come for the people of this country, which is not only the wealthiest per capita on the face of the earth, but one of the best enlightened per capita, to make known to the world that we have learned an inescapable fact: That is that America, with or without her consent, has been thrust by Almighty God to a position of leadership in the world. Down through the centuries there have been just two ways by which men, either singly or in organized groups, have exerted influence. One way is by *brute force*, which in our case would mean overwhelming military might at our fingertips during the years ahead; the other is by strong *moral leadership*, by precept and example, by strong and unswerving allegiance and support to the accepted idea or philosophy.

We have already proved rather conclusively to ourselves that we do not intend to elect the first course. We have destroyed our military machine with such rapidity and to such an extent that it is now a mockery as a fighting force; and still we clamor and rail that it is not more completely destroyed. It is not surprising that we have discarded this first method of insuring peace in the world, although our hysterical and selfish yodeling is not to be condoned. This method has always been diametrically opposed to the basic American character. All of our history has shown that the American people will not tolerate any potent or effective military force in peacetime. And although I firmly believe that after this postwar hysteria has died down the citizens of this country will be rather thoroughly ashamed of themselves, I do not believe that we will see fit to maintain a military force which would be adequate to our position, as based on the philosophy of peace by force in the hands of a peace-loving nation.

But as for the second idea, and by far the more challenging idea, what can the average American citizen honestly say that he has contributed—by his personal conduct and outlook—to the undoubtedly right and sound method since the end of the war? We need not kid ourselves that the one hundred and thirty odd million individuals in this country can go on thinking entirely in personal, restricted terms, and that anything lasting or worthwhile will have been achieved by this war.

There have been forms of government in the world, some recently extinct, which did not reflect—or reflected only partially—the will, desires, and the character of the people they represented, because the people did not have a voice in these governments. History has shown that in most cases the character of the governments were more malevolent, or cruel, or treacherous than the basic nature of the people they represented. But there has never been a case in history, to my knowledge, where the government was *better* than the people, or where it exerted any influence for good that was not reflective of the desires and the expressed wishes of the governed.

I believe that the face which America shows the world will always be the composite face of the majority of her citizens; that the lines of character thereon will delineate with unmistakable accuracy the character of her citizenry; will reflect their thinking and their attitude toward life.

Thus far in our postwar era, we have been guilty of attempting to deceive ourselves. We have tried to deceive ourselves that our postwar responsibilities could be discharged without painful and heavy sacrifices from us as a nation and from us as individuals. We have told ourselves on the one hand that we have great and grave responsibilities and on the other hand that these responsibilities and these tasks could be discharged without sacrifice and personal cost to us as citizens. As a nation, we have committed the one great and damning sin which will destroy an individual character—the sin of self-delusion. We who know that war demands and extracts the guts and blood and sinews and muscles of young men have thought that we could buy off with a song the demands that come with the aftermath of war.

Though the physical tasks that have faced us since the end of war have been staggering, they have been nothing as compared to what faced us in war. Yet we have not done them as well, or half as well. Why? It is plainly and simply because we, as a people—we and most of our leaders—have all during the course of the struggle deliberately and systematically deluded ourselves into thinking that the end of the war would mean the end of restraint, the end of discipline. We have not said that it would bring the end of responsibility, but we have been guilty of wishful and extremely hazy and nebulous thinking as to how the responsibility would be carried out. We knew what the war demanded, and we gave. But somehow, we have thought that from here on, everybody could ride free: that all our veterans could come home immediately, and no one would have to replace them; that everyone could continue to receive wartime wage for a peacetime work schedule, and no one would have to pay the difference; that we could leave half a world to starve and still retain our prestige as big brothers of the universe; that we could settle all our problems now on the basis of who can shout the loudest, whereas a few short months ago, some measure of restraint was recognized as essential.

If there has been one elemental truth hammered at mankind through bloody ages, it is that men must pay for the simple right to live peaceably, either by periodic wars or by continuing hard work for peace. This nation has repeatedly proved to the world that we can do prodigious things in preparing for and fighting a war once it is upon us. We have proved beyond question that a truly democratic nation can be the most powerful and fearful on earth once it is aroused and prepared for war, once the people of that nation have united for a common purpose. We know, and the world knows, that the reason for this is that the free men of this country have, by and large, willingly imposed self-discipline and such hardships and restrictions as were necessary to defeat the common enemy. But we have yet to show ourselves or the world that the free men of this nation can continue this self-imposed discipline and personal sacrifice, either in individual mental attitude or in fact and action, for as much as one week after the end of a war. From the sounding of the last shot, the attitudes of the majority of people change instantly from one of voluntary restraint to something which is strictly the reverse. This, to me, is a far more significant thing than the fact that we are always caught unprepared for war. It is to the credit of our national character as a peace-loving people, though not necessarily to our national intelligence, that the latter is always the case. Our fault is at the end of war, not the beginning. And it is to our everlasting discredit that the one nation in the world, which is empowered above all others to demonstrate democracy in action, must make the same old mistake, over and over again.

There is no loss of faith in the essential goodness of human nature involved in recognizing this fact. I, personally, have come out of my limited experiences in this war with an increased faith in my fellow man. Despite all the rottenness in human nature, I have seen what individual men can and will do when they are faced with a clear-cut responsibility. I know that, despite the inevitable failures, the American citizen-soldier did unparalleled things, willingly and unselfishly, both in the battle and behind the battle, and that the great majority of his fellow Americans were conscientiously backing him, in whatever capacities they served. Despite all the exceptions, all the mistakes, and all the individual failures, these things are unmistakably true.

And I thrill to a nation that will shower one hundred thousand dollars into the lap of a wounded veteran who wants to establish a chicken farm for his future. I am proud of a people who will pour gifts of all descriptions, from all parts of the land, into the hospital room of a veteran whose plaster-sheathed body appeared on the cover of a news magazine; who will pour ransom money into the hands of a young couple whose child has been reportedly held by kidnappers for money. I cherish above all things that innate spontaneity of thought and action, that instantaneous and uninhibited reaction of Americans to something that we should have anticipated but, having failed, must find at the last hour.

*   *   *

There is an angle of superficial and false thinking voiced much of late which seems to typify the general weakness and the great danger. How many times have we heard such well-meaning words as these: veterans have a right to *demand* a lasting peace; veterans have the right to *demand* homes, high wages, benefits of this or that nature? As I have read some of these sentiments, they seem to suggest something over and above the proper and expected considerations, which we know are due the veterans of this war. They seem to suggest that the veteran is someone who is to come home from the wars and demand an accounting of the past and future from the thoroughly confused citizenry of this country.

I do not believe that the majority of veterans sponsor this feeling, even taking into consideration that there are among us a reasonable proportion of rotters who did not undergo any magical change under fire, and that the rest of us are laboring under the postwar hysteria and irresponsibility which grips the whole country. I believe that the average veteran holds himself fully accountable for one citizen's responsibility for our country's future, even though all of us seem to have temporarily lost sight of some very elementary issues.

If the combat veteran is to discharge his future obligations to this country and to the world, if he is to live courageously and with a measure of unselfishness, how else than applying those simple truths which he may have discovered in the high moments of conflict? The man who has been in battle—on land, sea, or in the air—has had a unique opportunity to know his innate manhood and his inescapable relation to mankind, stripped of all extraneous influences, faced with elemental issues of life and death. In a compressed lifetime of experience—wherever or however it came—he was forced to discover himself for what he basically was and to know how he was related to fellow mankind. What he may have slowly and painfully learned in a normal lifetime, he was forced to learn in a relatively short time, and under unnatural circumstances. He discovered within himself inner recesses of fortitude which he never knew existed and between himself and others inevitable bands of kinship which had hitherto been unknown to him.

The basic problem of readjustment—about which we have rightfully concerned ourselves—centers around a man's effort to transpose his wartime discoveries about himself and the rest of mankind to his peacetime pursuits, whatever they may be.

We do not pretend here to know or understand fully the experiences which may have come to men in other forms of combat. Yet the hard core of fear could have been the same in all, for Death is a terrible thing for young men to face, whenever it comes; and all other things could have been irrelevant and of lesser note. When it was faced with prior knowledge, all our future—what might have been our future—seemed ridiculously simple and easy to live. Perhaps for glorious, terrible moments we had caught a glimpse of the elemental simplicity of life, and we had seen for a space how inextricably it was bound with death.

Why did my friend die, and why did I live? This is the basic dual question which haunts the men who return from combat. It has come back with us to all parts of the land—to the villages, the small towns, the great cities, and the open, peaceful countryside in north, south, east, and west. Men will face it and ask it within themselves in all currents of American life. To recognize the query and leave it unanswered, we condemn our souls to death in life and exist throughout the years in defeated bitterness, skepticism, and disillusionment. We must live the answer, now and in the years ahead, or there is scant hope for the world.

And yet, for young men, it is not easy. The transition is difficult, and the way is not always clear.

Each day of combat was a lifetime in itself, a beginning and an ending. Each day we flew a mission, we fulfilled a clear-cut purpose and an unquestionably right and necessary end. The issues of our lives were simple and unmistakable and, for the time being, our destinies were clear. Those who could forget the fear of death or overcome it had a God-given satisfaction not always known in ordinary life. This was achievement. This was purpose accomplished. This was destiny fulfilled.

Some who rose to those high moments may falter in the quieter ways of normal living. Men who excelled on this plateau of existence may stumble among the little perplexities of life as it normally is. Some who could have died at a pinnacle of personal unselfishness and spiritual fulfillment may lose themselves in quieter ways. Some who took the Hand of God and moved into the realm of death unafraid may forget his help and quail at lesser issues. Men who once could see their small personal efforts in relation to our nation's destiny and the destiny of mankind may lose sight of them in years to come; may fail in citizenship to our nation and our world.

Lest these things should come to pass, they should remember. For in remembering, they can renew faith.

For Christ's sake, top turret, remember the day when you struggled back through your broken, staggering plane without your parachute and gave first aid—and life—to your wounded brother? You forgot yourself, and you were the Good Samaritan, whom you had read about as a child.

Remember the time, copilot, when you stayed with your plane and brought it home—God knows how—because your pilot was wounded and could not bail out? You were your brother's keeper then.

Do you remember, navigator, that day, years ago now, when your plane was shattered and you were wounded, high over Germany? Do you remember that you scrawled a heading for home on a scrap of paper with a broken pencil and hand—that, weak and fainting as you were, you forced all but your burning purpose into the background and did your job?

That day, you loved duty more than life, and your fellowmen more than yourself.

You can look at that boy of yours, engineer, and remember well the day he was born. You were over the target that day, doing your job, forgetting yourself.

And pilot, remember that morning when radio was missing at the mission breakfast? You sat down to eat, and for the first time, you couldn't enjoy your breakfast. Because you were worried about him. Because you were disappointed in him and knew that you would have to punish him. Then he came in to you at the mess hall, looking like a downcast puppy, with black eye and disheveled uniform, and asked if he could fly the mission with you and the crew. He had been in a fight at a pub and had been arrested by the MPs. He had been in their custody since early last night and had been brought to the base just before breakfast time. He had rushed from the orderly room down to the mess hall to catch you before briefing. And now he stood before you, ashamed, eager to go out with you and the crew to certain danger, perhaps to death. He wanted to go more than anything else in the world. And you were glad to have him. You welcomed him, and you finished your breakfast with a new gusto. You flew that mission together, and a new niche was carved in your memory of ten men banded together for a short time that might have been forever.

And remember the day—all of you—when you led a combat box over the target and dropped the bombs. At first, you thought you had missed. And there, even there over Germany, disappointment fell over you like a pall. Then you feared failure more than death. Then you were men.

And now, surely you must know. For those who died this may yet be a fulfillment of destiny. For us who live, a test for living.

Col. James F. Risher, Jr.
USAF (retired)

b. May 8, 1916-d. July 22, 1986

BIBLIOGRAPHY

(Forward Section of the Book)

Astor, Gerald. *The Mighty Eighth*. Random House, 1997.

Borne, Walter F. *Clash of Wings*. Touchstone, 1997.

Caidin, Martin. *Flying Forts*. Ballantine Books, 1969.

Cherny, Arnold. *The Candy Bombers*. G. P. Putnam and Sons, 2008.

Closway, Captain Gordon R., editor and compiler. Pictorial Record of the 401st Bomb Group, 401st Bomb Group Association. Newsfoto Publishing Co., San Angelo, Texas.

Collier, Richard. *Bridge Across The Sky*. McGraw-Hill, 1978.

Darlow, Stephen. *D-Day Bombers*. Grub Street-London, U.K., 2004.

Doolittle, General James H., with Carol V. Glines. *I Could Never Be So Lucky Again*. Bantam Books, 1991.

Dorr, Robert F. *Mission to Berlin*. MBI Publishing, 2011.

Jablonski, Edward. *Double Strike*. Doubleday and Co., 1974.

Maslen, Vic. *614th Bombardment Squadron*. (H) History, 1986.

Miller, Donald L. *Masters of the Air*. Simon and Schuster, 2006.

Morrison, William. *Fortress Without A Roof*. St. Martin's Press, 1982.

Mrazek, Robert J. *To Kingdom Come*. NAL Caliber, 2011.

Nichol, John, and Tony Rennel. *Tail-End Charlies: The Last Battles of the Bomber War, 1944-1945*. St. Martin's Press, 2008.

Risher, Col. James F., Jr. (USAF, ret.). Summer Diary, 1944, a draft undated manuscript. unpublished.

Risher, Col. James F., Jr. (USAF ret.). Major J. F. Risher: Miscellaneous Correspondence and Writings. unpublished (circa 1948).

Schuller, Bill, editor. *401st Bomb Group: The Best Damned Outfit in the USAAF*. Turner Publishing Co., 2000.

Stout, Jay A. *Fortress Ploesti: The Campaign to Destroy Hitler's Oil*. Casemate, 2003.

CPSIA information can be obtained at www.ICGtesting.com
Printed in the USA
LVOW090918120612

285711LV00001B/10/P